I0020032

IOT Based Simple and efficient projects
using Arduino, Raspberry pi NAS Server,
Node MCU ESP8266 and Cloud Platforms

© Anbazhagan.k

IOT Based Simple and efficient projects using Arduino,
Raspberry pi, Node MCU ESP8266 and Cloud Platforms

Contents at a Glance   **PageNo**

1. Acknowledgments   3

2. Introduction   4

3. Dumpster Monitoring using
    Arduino & ESP8266   6

4. Web Controlled IoT Notice
    Board using Raspberry Pi   21

5. Raspberry Pi Microwave   37

6. How to build Raspberry Pi NAS
    Server using Samba   43

7. Log Temperature Sensor Data to Google
    Sheet using NodeMCU ESP8266   54

8. Lora Based GPS Tracker using
    Arduino and LoRa Shield   87

9. How to install Node-RED on
    Raspberry Pi to Control an LED 109

10. MQTT Based Raspberry Pi Home Automation:
    Controlling Raspberry Pi GPIO using MQTT
    Cloud   136

11. Node.js with Arduino: Controlling Brightness of
    LED through Web Interface   147

12. How to Use Deep Sleep Mode in ESP8266 for
    Power Saving   171

Acknowledgments

The writer might want to recognize the diligent work of the article group in assembling this book. He might likewise want to recognize the diligent work of the Raspberry Pi Foundation and the Arduino bunch for assembling items and networks that help to make the Internet Of Things increasingly open to the overall population. Yahoo for the democratization of innovation!

Introduction

The Internet of Things (IOT) is a perplexing idea comprised of numerous PCs and numerous correspondence ways. Some IOT gadgets are associated with the Internet and some are most certainly not. Some IOT gadgets structure swarms that convey among themselves. Some are intended for a solitary reason, while some are increasingly universally useful PCs. This book is intended to demonstrate to you the IOT from the back to front. By structure IOT gadgets, the per user will comprehend the essential ideas and will almost certainly develop utilizing the rudiments to make his or her very own IOT applications. These included ventures will tell the per user the best way to assemble their very own IOT ventures and to develop the models appeared. The significance of Computer Security in IOT gadgets is additionally talked about and different systems for protecting the IOT from unapproved clients or programmers. The most significant takeaway from this book is in structure the tasks yourself.

1. Dumpster Monitoring using Arduino & ESP8266

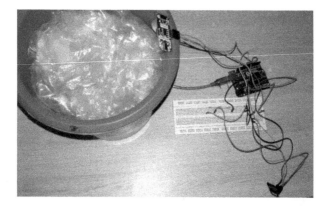

We are gonna to do an IOT based dumpster/trash Supervising System which will disclose us that if the junk can is unfilled or whole through the webserver as well as you can know the status of your 'Garbage Can' or 'Dumpsters' from anyplace on the planet over the Internet. It will be extremely helpful and can be introduced in the Trash Cans at open places just as at home.

In this IOT Project, a Ultrasonic Sensor is utilized for identifying whether the rubbish can is loaded up with trash or not. Here Ultrasonic Sensor is introduced at the peak point of Trash Can and will quantify the separation of trash from the peak point of Trash can and we can set a limit an incentive as per the size of garbage can. In that case the separation will be not as much as this limit esteem, implies that the Trash can is brimming with trash and we will print the message "Container is Full" on the website page and in the event that the separation will be more than this edge esteem, at that point we will print the message "Crate is Empty". Here we have set the Threshold opinion of 5cm in the Program code. We will use ESP8266 Wi-Fi module for associating the Arduino to the webserver. Here we have utilized Local webserver to show the functioning of this Trash Monitoring System.

Segments Required:

1. Arduino Uno (you can utilize some other)

2. ESP8266 Wi-Fi module

3. HC-SR04 Ultrasonic sensor

4. 1K Resistors

5. Breadboard

6. Associating wires

HC-SR04 Ultrasonic Sensor:

The Ultrasonic Sensor is used to quantify the division with high precision and consistance readings. It can gauge good ways since 20mm to 4000mm or since 1 inch to 13 feet. It emanates a ultrasound wave at the recurrence of 40KHz noticeable all around and on the off chance that the item will come in its manner, at that point it will bob return to the sensor. By utilizing that time which it takes to strike the article and returns, you can figure the separation.

The ultrasonic sensor have tetrad pins. Two are VCC as well as GND which will be associated with the 5V as well as the GND of the Arduino while the other two pins are Trig and Echo pins which will be associated with any advanced pins of Arduino. The trig stick will send the sign and the Echo stick will be utilized to get the sign. To produce a ultrasound signal, you should make the Trig stick higher for about 10us that will dispatch a octet cycle sonic blast at the speed of sound as well as on the basis of striking the article, it will be gotten by the Echo stick.

Further check underneath ventures to appropriately comprehend the working of Ultrasonic sensor and to quantify the separation of any item utilizing it:

1. Arduino Based Distance Measurement utilizing Ultrasonic Sensor
2. Separation Measurement utilizing HC-SR04 and AVR Microcontroller

ESP8266 Wi-Fi Module:

ESP8266 is a Wi-Fi module which will give your tasks access to Wi-Fi or web. It is a modest gadget yet it will make your ventures amazing. It can speak with any microcontroller and make the activities remote. It is in the rundown of most driving gadgets in the IOT stage. It keeps running on 3.3V in addition to that case you will give it 5V, at that point it will get harm.

The ESP8266 have octet sticks; the VCC as well as CH-PD will be associated with 3.3V to empower the Wi-Fi.

The TX as well as RX pins will be in charge of the correspondence of ESP8266 with the Arduino. The RX stick gets a shoot at 3.3V so you should create a voltage separator for it as we made in our venture.

Circuit Diagram and Explanation:

As a matter of first importance we will associate the ESP8266 with the Arduino. ESP8266 keeps running on 3.3V and on the off chance that you will give it 5V from the Arduino, at that point it won't work appropriately and it might get harm. Interface the VCC just as the CH_PD to the 3.3V stick of Arduino. The RX stick of ESP8266 manages 3.3V and it won't talk with the Arduino at whatever point we will interface it genuinely to the Arduino. Thusly, we should make a voltage divider for it. Three 1k resistors associated in arrangement will take every necessary step for us. Associate the RX to the stick 11 of the Arduino through the resistors as showed up in the diagram beneath and furthermore the TX of the Arduino to the stick 10 of the Arduino.

Presently it's an ideal opportunity to associate the HC-SR04 ultrasonic sensor with the Arduino. Associations of the ultrasonic sensor with the Arduino are straightforward.

Associate the VCC and the ground of the ultrasonic sensor to the 5V and the ground of the Arduino. At that point interface the TRIG as well as ECHO stick of ultrasonic sensor in the stick 8 as well as 9 of the Arduino separately.

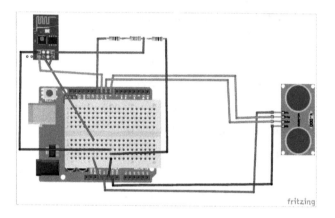

Code Explanation:

Before transferring the code, make sure that you are associated with the Wi-Fi of your ESP8266 gadget. You can check the full code in Code area underneath, code has been very much clarified by the remarks, further we have additionally clarified some significant capacities beneath.

The Arduino will initially peruse the Ultrasonic Sensor. It will send a ultrasonic sign at a speed of sound when we will make the TRIG stick high for 10us. The sign will rebound in the wake of striking the item and we will store the movement time length in the variable named term. At that point we will ascertain the separation of article (trash for our situation) by applying an equation and will store it in the variable named separation.

```
digitalWrite(trigPin, LOW);

delayMicroseconds(2);

digitalWrite(trigPin, HIGH);

delayMicroseconds(10);

digitalWrite(trigPin, LOW);

duration = pulseIn(echoPin, HIGH);

distance= duration*0.034/2;
```

For printing the yield on the site page in internet browser, we should utilize HTML programming. Along these lines, we have made a string named website page and put away the yield in it. To tell whether the junk can is vacant or not, we have connected a condition there. In the event that the separation will be under 5cm, at that point it will demonstrate "Bin is Full" on the website page and on the off chance that the separation will be more prominent than 5cm, at that point it will demonstrate the message "Crate is Empty" on site page.

```
if(esp8266.available())

{

    if(esp8266.find("+IPD,"))

    {

    delay(1000);

    int connectionId = esp8266.read()-48;

    String webpage = "<h1>IOT Garbage Monitoring Syst
em</h1>";
```

```
webpage += "<p><h2>";

if (distance<5)

{

webpage+= " Trash can is Full";

}

else{

   webpage+= " Trash can is Empty";

   }

webpage += "</h2></p></body>";
```

The accompanying code will send and demonstrate the information on the website page. The information, we put away in string named 'page', will be spared in string named 'order'. The ESP8266 will at that point read the character individually from the 'direction' and will print it on the page.

```
String sendData(String command, const int timeout, boole
an debug)

{

    String response = "";

    esp8266.print(command);

    long int time = millis();

    while( (time+timeout) > millis())

    {

      while(esp8266.available())

      {

      char c = esp8266.read();

      response+=c;

      }
```

```
}

if(debug)

{

   Serial.print(response);

}

   return response;

}
```

Testing and Output of the Project:

In the wake of transferring the code, open the Serial Monitor and it will demonstrate to you an IP address as demonstrated as follows.

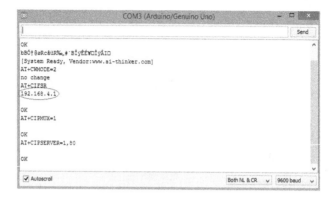

Type this IP address in your program, it will demonstrate to you the yield as demonstrated as follows. You should revive the page again in the event that you need to see again that the garbage can is vacant or not.

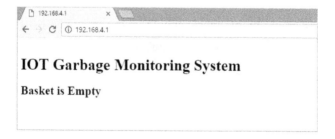

So this how this Garbage Monitoring System functions, this undertaking can be additionally improved by including couple of more highlights in it like we can set one more message when the Trash Can is half filled or we can trigger an Email/SMS to caution the client when Trash Basket is full.

Code :

```
#include <SoftwareSerial.h>        // including the library
for the software serial
#define DEBUG  true
SoftwareSerial  esp8266(10,11);     /* This will make the
pin 10 of arduino as RX pin and
pin 11 of arduino as the TX pin Which means that you
have to connect the TX from the esp8266
to the pin 10 of arduino and the Rx from the esp to the pin
11 of the arduino*/

const int trigPin = 8;        // Making the arduino's pin 8
as the trig pin of ultrasonic sensor
const int echoPin = 9;          // Making the arduino's pin 9
as the echo pin of the ultrasonic sensor
// defining two variable for measuring the distance
long duration;
int distance;
```

```
void setup()
{
  Serial.begin(9600);          // Setting the baudrate at 9600
  esp8266.begin(9600);         // Set the baudrate according
to you esp's baudrate. your esp's baudrate might be
different from mine
  pinMode(trigPin, OUTPUT);    // Setting the trigPin as
Output pin
  pinMode(echoPin, INPUT);     // Setting the echoPin as
Input pin

  sendData("AT+RST\r\n",2000,DEBUG);          //
command to reset the module
  sendData("AT+CWMODE=2\r\n",1000,DEBUG);     //
This will configure the mode as access point
  sendData("AT+CIFSR\r\n",1000,DEBUG);        // This
command will get the ip address
  sendData("AT+CIPMUX=1\r\n",1000,DEBUG);     //
This will configure the esp for multiple connections
  sendData("AT+CIPSERVER=1,80\r\n",1000,DEBUG);
// This command will turn on the server on port 80
}
void loop()
{
digitalWrite(trigPin, LOW);   // Making the trigpin as low
```

```
delayMicroseconds(2);        // delay of 2us
digitalWrite(trigPin, HIGH); // making the trigpin high for
10us to send the signal
delayMicroseconds(10);
digitalWrite(trigPin, LOW);
duration = pulseIn(echoPin, HIGH);   // reading the
echopin which will tell us that how much time the signal
takes to come back
distance= duration*0.034/2;        // Calculating the
distance and storing in the distance variable


 if(esp8266.available())        // This command will that
check if the esp is sending a message
 {
  if(esp8266.find("+IPD,"))
  {
   delay(1000);
   int connectionId = esp8266.read()-48;  /* We are
subtracting 48 from the output because the read() function
returns
                       the ASCII decimal value and
the first decimal number which is 0 starts at 48*/
   String webpage = "<h1>IOT Garbage Monitoring
System</h1>";
    webpage += "<p><h2>";
```

```
        if (distance<5)
        {
        webpage+= " Trash can is Full";
        }
        else{
        webpage+= " Trash can is Empty";
        }
      webpage += "</h2></p></body>";
    String cipSend = "AT+CIPSEND=";
    cipSend += connectionId;
    cipSend += ",";
    cipSend +=webpage.length();
    cipSend +="\r\n";
sendData(cipSend,1000,DEBUG);
    sendData(webpage,1000,DEBUG);
    String closeCommand = "AT+CIPCLOSE=";
    closeCommand+=connectionId;
    closeCommand+="\r\n";
    sendData(closeCommand,3000,DEBUG);
    }
  }
}


String sendData(String command, const int timeout,
boolean debug)
```

```
{
    String response = "";
    esp8266.print(command);
    long int time = millis();
    while( (time+timeout) > millis())
    {
        while(esp8266.available())
        {
            char c = esp8266.read();
            response+=c;
        }
    }
    if(debug)
    {
        Serial.print(response);
    }
    return response;
}
```

2.Web Controlled IoT Notice Board using Raspberry Pi

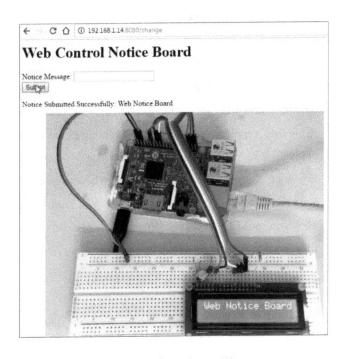

We as a whole know about the Wireless Notice Board as we have officially constructed Wireless Notice Board utilizing GSM and Arduino. Be that as it may, today we are proceeding and as opposed to utilizing GSM as remote medium, this time we are utilizing Internet to remotely send the message from Web Browser to the LCD which is associated with Raspberry Pi. As message is transmitted through the internet browser, so it very well may be sent utilizing Computer, PDA or tablet, so it will include one more undertaking in our IoT ventures accumulation.

In this Web Controlled Notice Board, we have made a neighborhood web server for exhibition, this can be a worldwide server over web. At the Raspberry Pi, we have utilized 16x2 LCD to show message and Flask for accepting the message over system. At whatever point Raspberry gets any remote message from Web program, it shows on the LCD. We will examine about these things in detail in this article.

Components Required:

1. Raspberry Pi 3 (any model)
2. Wi-Fi USB adapter (if not using Raspberry Pi 3)
3. 16x2 LCD
4. Bread Board
5. Power cable for Raspberry Pi
6. Connecting wires
7. 10K Pot

Working Explanation and Creating the WebPage:

In this undertaking, the principle segment is Raspberry Pi, which is the core of this task and used to control the procedures identified with this venture. Like: Driving LCD, getting "Notice messages" from the server and so forth.

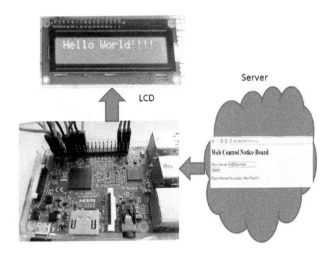

Here, we have made a web server, which gives an approach to send "Notice Message" to Raspberry Pi utilizing Flask in an internet browser. The Flask is a microframework for Python. This apparatus is Unicode based having worked

being developed server and debugger, coordinated unit testing support, support for secure treats and its simple to utilize, these things make it valuable for the specialist.

We have made a website page with a TextBox and a Submit catch, where we can enter our "Notice Message" in TextBox and after that submit it to the server by tapping on Submit catch. This web application is created by utilizing HTML language. The code of this site page is given beneath and extremely straightforward.

```
<h1>Web Control Notice Board (Welcome_friends)</h1>

</div>

<div data-role="content">

<form method="post" action="change">

  <label for="slider-1">Notice Message:</label>

  <input type="text" name="lcd" id="lcd" />

  <br />
```

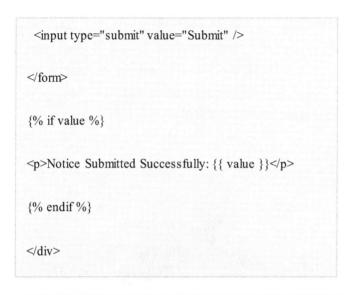

```
<input type="submit" value="Submit" />

</form>

{% if value %}

<p>Notice Submitted Successfully: {{ value }}</p>

{% endif %}

</div>
```

Client needs to duplicate glue the above given HTML code in some content tool (scratch pad) and spare the document with .HTML augmentation. At that point put this HTML record in a similar envelope where you have put your Python Code document (given toward the end) for this Web Controlled Notice Board. Presently you can simply run the Python code in Raspberry Pi, open the IP_address_of_your_Pi:8080 in internet Browser (like 192.168.1.14:8080) and info the message and snap submit, when you present the message, you will get the message on LCD associated with Raspberry Pi.

The site page is made utilizing HTML language, which contain a structure having a textbox and submit catch, with Heading (h1 tag) Web Control Notice Board. The structure has "change" is the activity that will be performed in code utilizing post strategy, when we click on Submit catch. The slider is hinder with mark "Notice Message".

After it, we can add a discretionary line to demonstrate the content which we have sent to the Raspberry Pi by means of the server.

```
{% if value %}

<p>Notice Submitted Successfully: {{ value }}</p>

{% endif %}
```

It checks the incentive in the content box and on the off chance that there is some an incentive in the textbox, at that point it prints the content on site page itself, with the goal that client can likewise observe the submitted message. Here 'esteem' is "input content or notice message" and we gonna type in slider box or content box.

Circuit Explanation:

Associations for this Wireless Message Board are extremely simple; we just need to interface LCD with the Raspberry Pi board by utilizing a few connectors over bread board. The client may utilize zero PCB for associations. RS, RW and EN pins of LCD are straightforwardly associated with stick 18, GND and 23. Furthermore, information pins of LCD D4, D5, D6, D7 are straightforwardly associated with Raspberry Pi's GPIO 24, 16, 20, 21. A 10K pot is utilized to control the splendor of LCD.

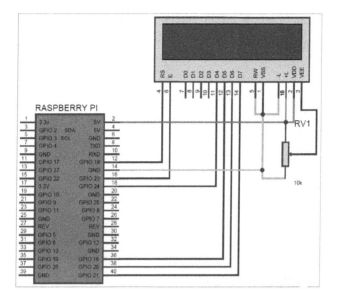

Additionally recollect, in the event that you don't have Raspberry Pi 3, you have to utilize the USB Wi-Fi connector for lower adaptation of Raspberry Pi as they don't have built in Wi-Fi like Raspberry Pi 3.

Programming Explanation and Flask:

We are utilizing Python language here for the Program. Prior to coding, client needs to arrange Raspberry Pi. You can check our past instructional exercises for Getting

Started with Raspberry Pi and Installing and Configuring Raspbian Jessie OS in Pi.

Before program Raspberry Pi, client needs to introduce a cup bolster bundle into the Raspberry Pi by utilizing given directions:

```
$ pip install Flask
```

After it we can run the Python program in the python supervisor of Raspberry Pi yet before this you have to supplant the IP address in Program with IP address of the Raspberry Pi. You can check IP address of the RPi board by utilizing ifconfig order:

```
Ifconfig
```

The programming some portion of this venture assumes a significant job to play out every one of the activities. As a matter of first importance, we incorporate required libraries for Flask, introduce factors and characterize pins for LCD.

```python
from flask import Flask

from flask import render_template, request

import RPi.GPIO as gpio

import os, time


app = Flask(__name__)


RS =18

EN =23

D4 =24

D5 =16

D6 =20

D7 =21

... ......
```

....

For LCD, def lcd_init() work is utilized to introduce LCD in four piece mode, def lcdcmd(ch) work is utilized for sending direction to LCD, def lcddata(ch) work is utilized for sending information to LCD as well as def lcdstring(Str) work is utilized to send information string to LCD. You can check every one of the capacities in Code given thereafter.

Beneath some portion of the Program is utilized to send the message from the internet browser to Raspberry Pi utilizing Flask.

```
@app.route("/")

def index():

    return render_template('web.html')

@app.route("/change", methods=['POST'])

def change():
```

```python
if request.method == 'POST':

    # Getting the value from the webpage

    data1 = request.form['lcd']

    lcdcmd(0x01)



    lcdprint(data1)

    return render_template('web.html', value=data1)



if __name__ == "__main__":

    app.debug = True

    app.run('192.168.1.14', port=8080,debug=True)
```

So this is the manner by which we can send the message from our PC or cell phone to the Raspberry Pi LCD and can make an IoT based Wireless Notice Board controlled over Web. Check the Full Python Code

Code

```
from flask import Flask
from flask import render_template, request
import RPi.GPIO as gpio
import os, time
app = Flask(__name__)
RS =18
EN =23
D4 =24
D5 =16
D6 =20
D7 =21
HIGH=1
LOW=0
OUTPUT=1
INPUT=0
gpio.setwarnings(False)
```

```python
gpio.setmode(gpio.BCM)
gpio.setup(RS, gpio.OUT)
gpio.setup(EN, gpio.OUT)
gpio.setup(D4, gpio.OUT)
gpio.setup(D5, gpio.OUT)
gpio.setup(D6, gpio.OUT)
gpio.setup(D7, gpio.OUT)
def begin():
  lcdcmd(0x33)
  lcdcmd(0x32)
  lcdcmd(0x06)
  lcdcmd(0x0C)
  lcdcmd(0x28)
  lcdcmd(0x01)
  time.sleep(0.0005)


def lcdcmd(ch):
  gpio.output(RS, 0)
  gpio.output(D4, 0)
  gpio.output(D5, 0)
  gpio.output(D6, 0)
  gpio.output(D7, 0)
  if ch&0x10==0x10:
    gpio.output(D4, 1)
  if ch&0x20==0x20:
```

```python
  gpio.output(D5, 1)
if ch&0x40==0x40:
  gpio.output(D6, 1)
if ch&0x80==0x80:
  gpio.output(D7, 1)
gpio.output(EN, 1)
time.sleep(0.0005)
gpio.output(EN, 0)
# Low bits
gpio.output(D4, 0)
gpio.output(D5, 0)
gpio.output(D6, 0)
gpio.output(D7, 0)
if ch&0x01==0x01:
  gpio.output(D4, 1)
if ch&0x02==0x02:
  gpio.output(D5, 1)
if ch&0x04==0x04:
  gpio.output(D6, 1)
if ch&0x08==0x08:
  gpio.output(D7, 1)
gpio.output(EN, 1)
time.sleep(0.0005)
gpio.output(EN, 0)
```

```python
def lcdwrite(ch):
    gpio.output(RS, 1)
    gpio.output(D4, 0)
    gpio.output(D5, 0)
    gpio.output(D6, 0)
    gpio.output(D7, 0)
    if ch&0x10==0x10:
        gpio.output(D4, 1)
    if ch&0x20==0x20:
        gpio.output(D5, 1)
    if ch&0x40==0x40:
        gpio.output(D6, 1)
    if ch&0x80==0x80:
        gpio.output(D7, 1)
    gpio.output(EN, 1)
    time.sleep(0.0005)
    gpio.output(EN, 0)
    # Low bits
    gpio.output(D4, 0)
    gpio.output(D5, 0)
    gpio.output(D6, 0)
    gpio.output(D7, 0)
    if ch&0x01==0x01:
        gpio.output(D4, 1)
    if ch&0x02==0x02:
```

```python
    gpio.output(D5, 1)
  if ch&0x04==0x04:
    gpio.output(D6, 1)
  if ch&0x08==0x08:
    gpio.output(D7, 1)
  gpio.output(EN, 1)
  time.sleep(0.0005)
  gpio.output(EN, 0)

def lcdprint(Str):
  l=0;
  l=len(Str)
  for i in range(l):
    lcdwrite(ord(Str[i]))
begin()
lcdprint("Welcome")
lcdcmd(0xc0)
lcdprint("Welcomes You")
time.sleep(5)
@app.route("/")
def index():
    return render_template('web.html')
@app.route("/change", methods=['POST'])
def change():
  if request.method == 'POST':
```

```python
    # Getting the value from the webpage
    data1 = request.form['lcd']
    lcdcmd(0x01)
    lcdprint(data1)
  return render_template('web.html', value=data1)
if __name__ == "__main__":
   app.debug = True
   app.run('192.168.1.14', port=8080,debug=True)
```

3. IoT Based Raspberry Pi Microwave

Microwave is an incredible creation and now it's turned into the piece of our regular daily existence. Nathan Broadbent have taken the Microwave to a totally new level and made it a top of the line IoT based gadget. Presently you can work the Microwave with your voice, or with your iPad or even from the Internet. Nathan hacked the Microwave all around shrewdly, supplanted its touch cushion hardware and included some extremely cool highlights with lovely sounds for notices and cautions. These every single insightful component have been fueled by Raspberry Pi at the back end, so it moves toward becoming Raspberry Pi Microwave.

This Raspberry Pi Microwave can tune in to your voice directions and can set the cooking time in like manner, its clock is consequently matched up with the Internet and you can have the equivalent touchpad in your telephone or PC so you can control it from your telephone. What's more, the coolest element of this Microwave is this, that you can simply filter the scanner tag of the item being cooked and place it in the Microwave, it will consequently get the guidelines from the 'online DB' and cook it as needs, you doesn't want to set anything. Nathan made an Online Microwave Cooking Database where you can include any item with its cooking directions and after that you simply need to examine it with standardized identification scanner appended to Microwave. Aside from that it can 'Tweet' when your sustenance is prepared.

Nathan truly worked superbly, he made another PCB plan for his Touchpad circuit and fitted it pleasantly in the Microwave board. He likewise improved the touchpad interface by evacuating some infrequently utilized capacities and structured another excellent Touchpad spread.

A USB center point is utilized to control the Raspberry Pi and other USB gadgets which has been utilized in this Microwave like USB fueled speaker, USB amplifier, Wi-Fi connector, and standardized tag scanner. The USB center is controlled by the Microwave power source itself utilizing a power connector.

All the item for this IoT Microwave is running over this Raspberry Pi and can be downloaded from the Nathen's GitHub account. Program is written in C language and can be utilized in Raspberry Pi utilizing the WiringPi library. All the product and different directions have been clarified well by Nathan, similar to he has utilized Sinatra application for web interface and PocketSphinx for Voice acknowledgment and made an online database for standardized identification scanner.

Despite the fact that it's very perplexing to hack and modify this Pi Microwave yet the outcomes are wonderful. At last Nathan cooked the genuine Raspberry Pie in Raspberry Pi Microwave

4. How to build Raspberry Pi NAS Server using Samba

Raspberry Pi is the pocket estimated PC having practically all the component of a typical PC including USB port, LAN port, sound/video yield, HDMI port and so on. It likewise has inbuilt Bluetooth and Wi-Fi availability which makes it ideal contender to fabricate different online servers like Webserver, Media server, Print Server, Plex server and so on. Here we make another server utilizing Raspberry Pi-File Server or NAS (Network Attached Storage), where you want to plug any capacity gadget with Raspberry Pi and access it utilizing any PC associated on a similar system. Utilizing NAS, you can share and access the records and organizers without really interfacing the capacity gadget to your framework.

There are different techniques to make Raspberry pi a NAS box. One of the strategy is to introduce circle picture of OpenMediaVault (OMV) and NAS4Free. They are accessible for nothing and can be effectively introduced by consuming the crisp picture into SD card, however along these lines the first Raspbian OS will be lost. Once introduced, without quite a bit of a stretch access media utilizing straightforward electronic UI just by entering IP address of the Pi in internet browser.

In this instructional exercise, we will introduce Samba in preinstalled Raspbian OS, so you don't need to free the default Raspbian OS. Samba is a re-usage of the SMB (Server Message Block) organizing convention which coordinates Linux PCs with MAC and Windows based frameworks. There is another convention named CIFS which is an execution of the SMB convention. These days, CIFs or SMB is utilized reciprocally, yet the vast majority utilize the term SMB.

Samba record server is anything but difficult to arrangement, which makes it perhaps the best answer for setting up a NAS, particularly with Windows machine. So here we will introduce and design Samba on Raspberry Pi to make it a File server.

Requirements

1. Raspberry Pi with Raspbian OS installed in it.

2. Any external storage like harddrive, SD card (optional)

Here, we will utilize SSH to get to Raspberry Pi on the workstation. You can utilize VNC or Remote Desktop association on the workstation, or can interface your Raspberry pi with a screen utilizing HDMI link.

Setting up Samba File Server on Raspberry Pi

1. Before introducing SMB bundles ensure our Raspberry pi is forward-thinking by running update direction.

```
sudo apt-get update

sudo apt-get upgrade
```

2. Presently introduce Samba bundles utilizing beneath direction.

```
sudo apt-get install samba samba-common-bin
```

3. At that point make an organizer and offer it on Network stockpiling. This envelope can be anyplace including the outer stockpiling gadgets. In this instructional exercise, we will make an envelope in "pi" client however it very well may be made in outer gadget associated with pi utilizing same strides as referenced beneath.

```
mkdir /home/pi/shared
```

4. Presently, share this organizer utilizing samba server. To arrangement this we need to adjust samba config document "smb.conf". This

document contains every one of the settings for sharing the media.

Open the document utilizing beneath order

sudo nano /etc/samba/smb.conf

5. In this record search for "##### Authentication #####" and just underneath glue following line.

security = user

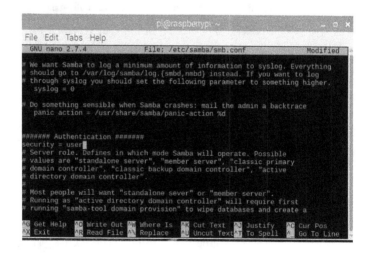

Presently, go to base of this document and glue the accompanying lines

[NAS]

path = /home/pi/shared

writeable=Yes

create mask=0777

directory mask=0777

public=no

[NAS] characterizes the location and different setups identified with the mutual envelopes. For instance, the mutual envelopes will be at the accompanying location:/raspberrypi/NAS and this location will be utilized in later advances while looking through the accessible system in Windows PC.

"way" – This alternative contains the location of the catalog that will be shared.

"writeable" – This choice enable the client to include documents in the organizer, on the off chance that this choice is set to indeed, at that point anybody can write in this envelope.

"make cover" and "index veil"– This choice characterizes the consents for both the records and envelopes and setting this to 0777 enables clients to peruse, compose, and execute.

"open" – This choice used to offer consent to any client to get to the envelopes and on the off chance that this is set to "no" at that point Raspberry Pi need a legitimate client to concede access to shared organizers.

6. Presently, spare the document "smb.conf" utilizing ctrl+x and hit enter. Next, make a client for Samba server on Pi to make an association with the mutual system drive.

We will make a client named "pi" (you can name it anything) and set a secret phrase anything you desire. Run the accompanying order to arrangement the client.

```
sudo smbpasswd -a pi
```

7. As a last advance, restart the samba administration to stack the arrangement changes. Run following order to restart samba.

```
sudo systemctl restart smbd
```

Presently, for sharing records and envelopes ensure you have associated Raspberry Pi with same Wi-Fi arrange as your workstation/PC is associated.

Connecting Windows to Raspberry Pi Samba Server

1. To access records and organizers on windows framework, we need to put the location of the mutual media. Go to My PC/This PC and snap on Computer tab and snap on the alternative named "Guide system drive" as demonstrated as follows.

2. Presently, put the location as \\raspberrypi\NAS (supplant NAS with the name that you have surrendered

while setting samba on pi) in Folder choice and snap on Finish as demonstrated as follows. In the event that the association comes up short, enter the pi's IP address instead of raspberrypi in the location. You can discover IP address utilizing the direction "hostname – I".

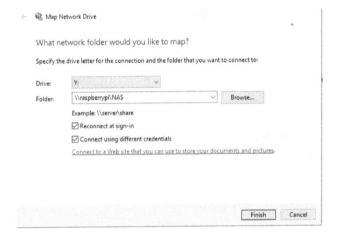

3. Next, enter the accreditations that you arrangement already utilizing smbpasswd. In the model I set the client name as pi and secret key as raspberry.

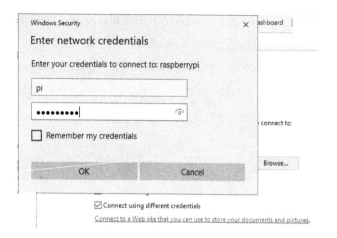

4. Presently, you can see the common system and the records in the mutual organizer as demonstrated as follows. You can reorder anything in this envelope and it will reflect in the Raspberry pi moreover.

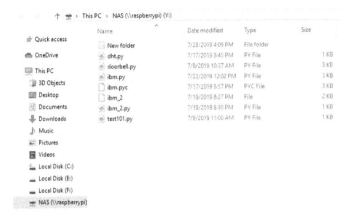

Any outside gadget like Hard Disk or SD card can be shared over the system just by following the above advances.

So this is the manner by which Raspberry Pi can be transformed into a continually running File server.

5. Log Temperature Sensor Data to Google Sheet using NodeMCU ESP8266

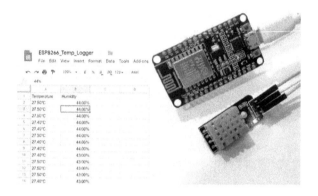

There are numerous IoT mists accessible to store and screen the information from different sensors. With expanding notoriety of IoT, increasingly number of sensors are utilized each day and these sensors produce unknown information which are valuable to control different gadgets on the IoT arrange. These information can be concentrated further and used to change structure or improve the framework execution. The Applications of Data Logging is tremendous and can be connected in Research Centers,

Scientific Labs, Operation Theaters, Patient Monitoring System and some more.

Today we will complete a comparative task and utilize the Google sheet as IoT cloud to log the information produced by a Temperature Sensor. Here we will utilize ESP8266 NodeMCU to send the temperature and moistness information from DHT11 sensor to the Google Sheet over the web. In past tasks we figured out how to log the information on SD card and other IoT mists like ThingSpeak, Amazon Web administrations (AWS), MQTT server, Adafruit IO, Firebase and so on.

This Google Sheet Logger framework is quite easy to learn and doesn't contain much peripherals. The Components are likewise lot of the time utilized. Note that, the dynamic web association is required to send the information to Google Sheet.

Components Required

1.   NodeMCU ESP8266 Module

2.   Jumpers

3. DHT11 Sensor

Circuit Diagram

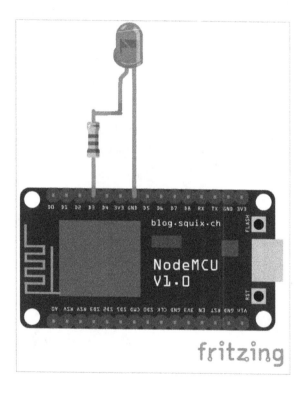

There is a couple of ventures before beginning to program ESP8266 for Logging Temperature Data on Google Sheet. We will require couple of certifications that will be utilized to convey and send the information from ESP8266 to Google Server to think about Google Sheet. The ESP8266 NodeMCU code is connected toward the part of the bargain.

I would prescribe to pursue the instructional exercise till the last as the instructional exercise is isolated into segments and each area will assume a significant job. Additionally the instructional exercise contains

Screenshots to enable you to better. The First step will get the Google Script ID from Google Sheet. For this, you have to pursue the beneath steps.

Creating Google Script in Google Sheet for Data Logging

1. Login to the Gmail with your Email ID and Password.

2. Click on App icon in the top most right corner highlighted in green circle and click on Docs.

3. The Google Docs screen will show up. Presently pick Sheets in the correct sidebar.

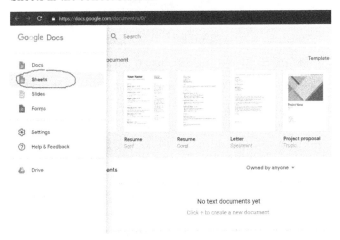

4. Make a New Blank Sheet.

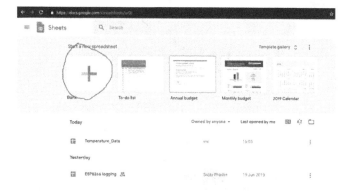

5. The Blank Sheet will be made with an "Untitled Spreadsheet". Simply rename this made Spreadsheet Project to any name you need. For my situation I have renamed "Untitled Spreadsheet" to "ESP8266_Temp_Logger" since I am logging temperature utilizing ESP8266. To rename the made Spreadsheet Project, go to "Document" > "Rename".

6. You can likewise include another different sheets in Google spread sheet. In this instructional exercise just one sheet is utilized. So we renamed "Sheet1" > "TempSheet" because we are logging Temperature information to sheet.

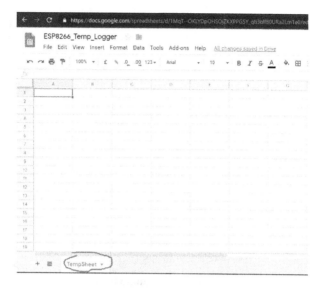

7. In the wake of renaming the made Spreadsheet Project and Sheet name, presently its opportunity to make a Google content.

8. Presently got to 'Devices' set apart in green circle and snap on "<> Script Editor" choice set apart on red circle.

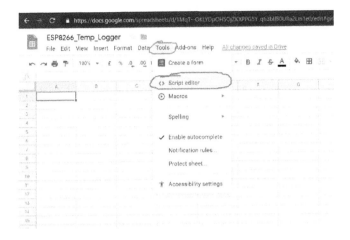

9. The new Google Script is made with "Untitled task". You can rename this Google Script File to any name you need. In this case we renamed to "Untitled venture" > "TempLog_Script".

10. Presently Copy and Paste the Google Script code from document connected in this ZIP record here (GoogleScript.gs). At that point alter the Sheet name and Sheet ID in the code. You can get the Sheet ID from the Sheet URL simply like demonstrated as follows. https://docs.google.com/spreadsheets/d/xxxxxxxxyyyyyyyz zzzzzzzz/edit#gid=0 , where "xxxxxxxxyyyyyyyzzzzzzzzz" is your Sheet ID.

11. When you reorder the Google Script then it will look like after.

TempLog_Script

12. Spare the document. On the off chance that you need to make your own sheet, at that point change your qualifications, for example, Sheet ID, Sheet Name and Sheet Project Name.

13. Presently we have wrapped the Setting up Google Script in Spreadsheet. Presently it's an ideal opportunity to get the significant qualification for example Google Script ID which will be written in the Arduino Program. On the off chance that you commit error in the duplicating Google Script ID, at that point the information won't reach to Google Sheet.

Getting the Google Script ID

1. Go to 'Distribute' > 'Send as Web App...'

2. The "Undertaking adaptation" will be "New". Select "your email id" in the "Execute the application as" field. Pick "Anybody, even mysterious" in the "Who approaches the application" field. And after that Click on "Convey". Note that When republishing please select the most recent form and afterward Deploy once more.

3. You should give the Google authorization to send it as web application. Simply click on "Survey Permissions".

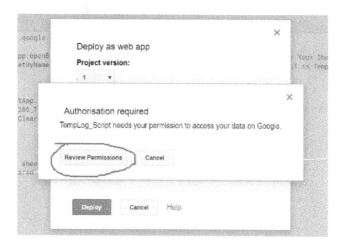

4. At that point pick your Email ID here utilizing which you have made spreadsheet.

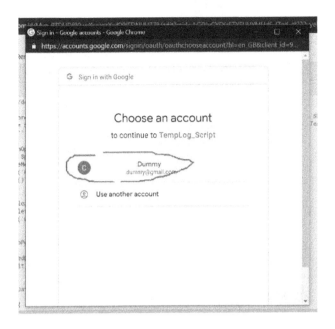

5. Snap on "Cutting edge".

6. And after that snap on "Go to 'your_script_name'(unsafe)". Here for my situation it is "TempLog_Script".

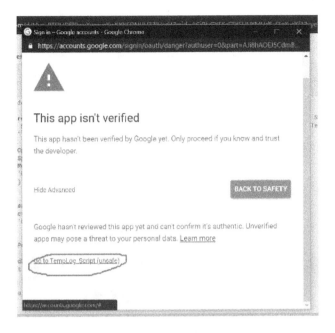

7. Snap on "Permit" and this will give the consent to send it as web application.

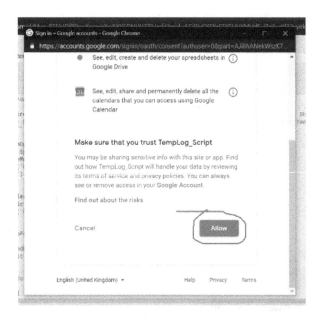

8. Presently you can view the new screen with a given connection and named as "Current web application URL". This URL contains Google Script ID. Simply duplicate the URL and free it some place.

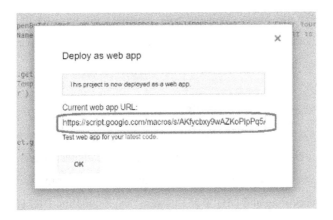

9. Presently when you duplicate the code, the configuration resembles _ScriptID___/exec>.

So here for my situation my Google content ID is "AKfycbxy9wAZKoPIpP53AvqYTFFn5kkqK_-avacf2NU_w7ycoEtlkuNt".

Simply spare this Google Script to some place.

Programming NodeMCU to Send Temperature Data to Google Sheets

Here the DHT sensor is associated with ESP8266 NodeMCU and ESP8266 NodeMCU is associated with Internet through WiFi to send the DHT11 readings to

Google Sheet. So begin with including the fundamental libraries. As common the total code is given toward the part of the arrangement.

The library ESP8266WiFi.h is utilized for getting to the elements of ESP8266, the HTTPSRedirect.h library is utilized for interfacing with Google Spreadsheet Server, DebugMacros.h is utilized to troubleshoot the information accepting and DHT.h is a used to the perused the DHT11 sensor.

```
#include <ESP8266WiFi.h>

#include "HTTPSRedirect.h"

#include "DebugMacros.h"

#include <DHT.h>
```

At first characterize the NodeMCU Pin Number where DHT11 sensor will be perused. Here the yield of DHT11 is associated with D4 of NodeMCU. Additionally characterize thee DHT type, here we are utilizing DHT11 sensor.

```
#define DHTPIN  D4

#define DHTTYPE  DHT11
```

Characterize factors to store the temperature and stickiness esteem.

```
float h;

float t;

String sheetHumid = "";

String sheetTemp = "";
```

Enter your WiFi certifications, for example, SSID name and Password.

```
const char* ssid= "Welcomefriends";

const char* password = "Welcomeuall";
```

Enter the Google server certifications, for example, have address, Google content ID and port number. The host and the port number is same as the connected code however you have to exchange the Google Scripts ID which we obtained from the above advances.

```
const char* host = "script.google.com";

const char* GScriptId = "AKfycbxy9wAZKoPIpPq5A
vqYTFxxxkkqK_avacf2NU_w7ycoEtlkuNt";

const int httpsPort = 443;
```

Characterize the URL of Google Sheet where the information will be composed. This is fundamentally a way where the information will be composed.

```
String url = String("/macros/s/") + GScriptId + "/exec
?value=Temperature";

String url2 = String("/macros/s/") + GScriptId + "/exe
c?cal";
```

Characterize the Google sheet address where we made the Google sheet.

```
String payload_base = "{\"command\": \"appendRow\", \
            \"sheet_name\": \"TempSheet\", \
            \"values\": ";
```

Characterize the customer to utilize it in the program ahead.

```
HTTPSRedirect* client = nullptr;
```

Begin the sequential debugger or screen at 115200 baud rate. You can likewise choose other baud rates, for example, 9600, 57600 and so forth. And after that initialise DHT11 sensor.

```
Serial.begin(115200);

dht.begin();
```

Associate with WiFi and trust that the association will set up.

```
WiFi.begin(ssid, password);

 while (WiFi.status() != WL_CONNECTED) {

  delay(500);

  Serial.print(".");

 }
```

Begin another HTTPS association. Note that in the case you are utilizing HTTPS the you have to compose the line setInscure() generally the association won't build up with server.

```
client = new HTTPSRedirect(httpsPort);

 client->setInsecure();
```

Start the respose body i.e. if the server replies then we can print it on serial monitor.

```
client->setPrintResponseBody(true);

client->setContentTypeHeader("application/json");
```

Associate with host. Here it is "script.google.com".

```
Serial.print("Connecting to ");

Serial.println(host);
```

Attempt association for multiple times and on the chance that doesn't interface in the wake of attempting multiple times, at that point drop the association.

```
bool flag = false;

for (int i = 0; i < 5; i++) {

  int retval = client->connect(host, httpsPort);

  if (retval == 1) {

    flag = true;
```

```
    break;

    }

    else

    Serial.println("Connection  failed. Retrying...");

    }
```

We will speak with server with GET and POST work. GET will be utilized to peruse the cells and POST will be utilized to compose into the cells. Get the cell information of A1 from Google sheet.

```
client->GET(url,  host);
```

Peruse the climate and moisture information from DHT11 sensor and spare it in factor. On the off chance that any peruses falls flat, at that point print a bomb message and return.

```
h = dht.readHumidity();
```

```
t = dht.readTemperature

if (isnan(h) || isnan(t)) {

    Serial.println(F("Failed to read from DHT sensor!")
);

    return;

}
```

Compose the information in the way. This information will be written in the Google Sheet. The information way contains Temperature and Humidity information, for example, sheetTemp and sheetHumid.

```
payload = payload_base + "\"" + sheetTemp + "," + sh
eetHumid + "\"}";
```

In the event that customer is associated, at that point basically send the Data to Google Sheet by utilizing POST work. Or in the same time spare it if the information neglects to send and check the disappointment.

```
if (client->POST(url2, host, payload)) {

  ;

}

else {

  ++error_count;

  DPRINT("Error-count while connecting: ");

  DPRINTLN(error_count);

}
```

In case that information sending fizzles for multiple times, at that point stop all procedures and exit and go to deepsleep.

```
if (error_count > 3) {

  Serial.println("Halting processor...");

  delete client;
```

```
    client = nullptr;

    Serial.printf("Final   free heap:  %u\n", ESP.getFree
Heap());

    Serial.printf("Final   stack: %u\n", ESP.getFreeCont
Stack());

    Serial.flush();

    ESP.deepSleep(0);

}
```

Give a postponement of in any event 2 seconds after each
perusing and sending as it is suggested by the DHT library
and HTTPSRedirect library.

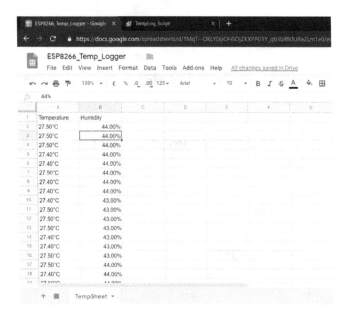

This completes the total instructional exercise on sending the sensor information to a Google sheet utilizing ESP8266.

Code

```
/*
 * ESP822  temprature logging to Google Sheet

*/
```

```cpp
#include <ESP8266WiFi.h>
#include "HTTPSRedirect.h"
#include "DebugMacros.h"
#include <DHT.h>
#define DHTPIN
D4                                          // what digital pin
we're connected to
#define DHTTYPE
DHT11                                       // select dht type
as DHT 11 or DHT22
DHT dht(DHTPIN, DHTTYPE);
float h;
float t;
String sheetHumid = "";
String sheetTemp = "";
const char* ssid = "Welcomefriends";        //replace
with our wifi ssid
const char* password = "welcomeuall";       //replace
with your wifi password
const char* host = "script.google.com";
const char *GScriptId =
"AKfycbxy9wAZKoPIpPq5AvqYTFFn5kkqK_-
avacf2NU_w7ycoEtlkuNt"; // Replace with your own
```

```
google script id
const int httpsPort = 443;  //the https port is same
// echo | openssls_client -connect script.google.com:443
|& opensslx509 -fingerprint -noout
const char* fingerprint = "";
//const uint8_t fingerprint[20] = {};
String url = String("/macros/s/") + GScriptId +
"/exec?value=Temperature";  // Write Teperature to
Google Spreadsheet at cell A1
// Fetch Google Calendar events for 1 week ahead
String url2 = String("/macros/s/") + GScriptId +
"/exec?cal";  // Write to Cell A continuosly
//replace with sheet name not with spreadsheet file name
taken from google
String payload_base = "{\"command\": \"appendRow\",\
          \"sheet_name\":\"TempSheet\",\
            \"values\":";
String payload = "";

HTTPSRedirect* client = nullptr;

// used to store the values of free stack and heap before
the HTTPSRedirect object is instantiated
// so that they can be written to Google sheets upon
instantiation
```

```
void setup() {
  delay(1000);
  Serial.begin(115200);
  dht.begin();    //initialise DHT11
Serial.println();
  Serial.print("Connecting to wifi: ");
  Serial.println(ssid);


  WiFi.begin(ssid, password);
  while (WiFi.status() != WL_CONNECTED)  {
    delay(500);
    Serial.print(".");
  }
  Serial.println("");
  Serial.println("WiFi connected");
  Serial.println("IP  address:");
  Serial.println(WiFi.localIP());
// Use HTTPSRedirect class to create a new TLS
connection
  client = new HTTPSRedirect(httpsPort);
  client->setInsecure();
  client->setPrintResponseBody(true);
  client->setContentTypeHeader("application/json");
  Serial.print("Connecting to ");
```

```cpp
  Serial.println(host);        //try to connect with
"script.google.com"
// Try to connect for a maximum of 5 times then exit
  bool flag = false;
  for (int i = 0; i < 5; i++) {
    int retval = client->connect(host, httpsPort);
    if (retval == 1) {
      flag = true;
      break;
    }
    else
      Serial.println("Connection failed. Retrying...");
  }
if (!flag) {
    Serial.print("Could not connect to server: ");
    Serial.println(host);
    Serial.println("Exiting...");
    return;
  }
// Finish setup() function in 1s since it will fire watchdog
timer and will reset the chip.
//So avoid too many requests in setup()
Serial.println("\nWrite into cell 'A1'");
    Serial.println("------>");
```

```
// fetch spreadsheet data
client->GET(url, host);

Serial.println("\nGET: Fetch Google Calendar Data:");
Serial.println("------>");
// fetch spreadsheet data
client->GET(url2, host);
Serial.println("\nStart Sending Sensor Data to Google
Spreadsheet");

// delete HTTPSRedirect object
delete client;
client = nullptr;
}
void loop() {
h = dht.readHumidity();                              //
Reading temperature or humidity takes about 250
milliseconds!
t = dht.readTemperature();                           //
Read temperature as Celsius (the default)
if (isnan(h) || isnan(t)) {                          //
Check if any reads failed and exit early (to try again).
Serial.println(F("Failed to read from DHT sensor!"));
return;
```

```
    }
    Serial.print("Humidity: ");  Serial.print(h);
    sheetHumid = String(h) +
String("%");                                    //convert integer
humidity to string humidity
    Serial.print("%  Temperature:
"); Serial.print(t);   Serial.println("Â°C ");
    sheetTemp = String(t) + String("Â°C");

static int error_count = 0;
    static int connect_count = 0;
    const unsigned int MAX_CONNECT  = 20;
    static bool flag = false;

payload = payload_base + "\"" + sheetTemp + "," +
sheetHumid + "\"}";

if (!flag) {
    client = new HTTPSRedirect(httpsPort);
    client->setInsecure();
    flag = true;
    client->setPrintResponseBody(true);
    client->setContentTypeHeader("application/json");
    }

if (client != nullptr) {
    if (!client->connected()) {
      client->connect(host, httpsPort);
```

```
    client->POST(url2,  host, payload, false);
    Serial.print("Sent : "); Serial.println("Temp and
Humid");
    }
  }
  else {
   DPRINTLN("Error  creating client object!");
   error_count = 5;
  }
if (connect_count > MAX_CONNECT)  {
   connect_count = 0;
   flag = false;
   delete client;
   return;
  }
//  Serial.println("GET  Data from cell 'A1':");
//  if (client->GET(url3,  host)) {
//    ++connect_count;
//  }
//  else {
//    ++error_count;
//    DPRINT("Error-count  while connecting: ");
//    DPRINTLN(error_count);
//  }
```

```
Serial.println("POST or SEND Sensor data to Google
Spreadsheet:");
  if (client->POST(url2, host, payload)) {
    ;
  }
  else {
    ++error_count;
    DPRINT("Error-count while connecting:");
    DPRINTLN(error_count);
  }
if (error_count > 3) {
    Serial.println("Halting processor...");
    delete client;
    client = nullptr;
    Serial.printf("Final free heap: %u\n",
ESP.getFreeHeap());
    Serial.printf("Final stack: %u\n",
ESP.getFreeContStack());
    Serial.flush();
    ESP.deepSleep(0);
  }

  delay(3000);    // keep delay of minimum 2 seconds as
dht allow reading after 2 seconds interval and also for
```

google sheet
}

6. Lora Based GPS Tracker using Arduino and LoRa Shield

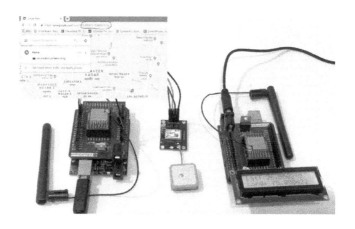

Knowing the whereabouts of a specific article/individual has consistently been soothing. Today, GPS is by and large widely utilized in resource the board applications like Vehicle Tracking, Fleet Tracking, Asset observing, Person following, Pet Tracker and so forth. For any GPS beacon the essential plan thought will be about its battery anticipation and checking range. Thinking about both, LoRa is by all accounts ideal decision since it has low power utilization and can work on long separations. Along these lines, in this instructional exercise we will construct GPS following framework utilizing LoRa, the framework will comprise of a Transmitter which will peruse the area data from the NEO-6M GPS module and transmit it remote over Lora. The recipient part will get the data and show it on a 16x2 LCD show. In the event that you are new to LoRa, at that point find out about LoRa and LoRaWAN Technology and how it tends to be interfaced with Arduino before continuing further.

To keep things basic and financially savvy for this task we won't utilize a LoRa entryway. Rather will perform distributed correspondence between the transmitter and beneficiary. Nevertheless, if you need a worldwide range you can supplant the beneficiary with a LoRa Gateway. Likewise since I am from India we will utilize the 433MHz LoRa module which is lawful ISM band here, consequently you may need to choose a module dependent on your nation. That being stated, how about we begin...

Materials Required

1. 433MHz Lora Antenna
2. Arduino Uno - 2Nos
3. NEO-6M GPS Module
4. SX1278 433MHz LoRa Module - 2

5. Arduino Lora Shield - 2Nos (PCB design available for download)
6. Connecting wires
7. LCD Display Module

Arduino LoRa Shield

To make building things with LoRa simpler, we have structured a LoRa Arduino Shield for this Project. This shield comprises of the SX1278 433MHz with a 3.3V controller structured utilizing LM317 Variable controller. The Shield will legitimately sit over Arduino giving it LoRa abilities. This LoRa Shield will prove to be useful when you need to convey LoRa detecting hubs or to make a LoRa work arrange. The total circuit chart for the LoRa Arduino Shield is given underneath

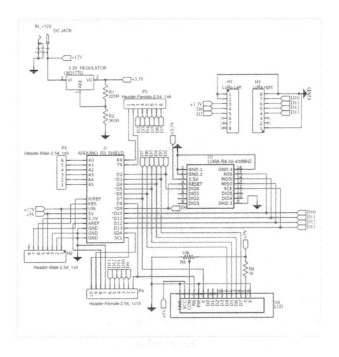

The Shield comprises of a 12V jack which when fueled will be utilized to manage 3.3V for the LoRa module utilizing the LM317 controller. It will likewise be utilized to control the Arduino UNO through Vin stick and the directed 5V from the Arduino is utilized to control the LCD on the shield. The yield voltage of the LM317 is fixed to be 3.3V utilizing the resistor R1 and R2 individually, the estimation of these resistors can be determined utilizing the LM317 Calculator.

Since the LoRa module expends extremely low power, it can likewise be controlled legitimately from the 3.3V stick of Arduino, yet we have utilized an outer controller structure since LM317 is more dependable than the on-board voltage controller. The shield additionally has a potentiometer which can be utilized to change the brilliance of the LCD. The association of LoRa module with Arduino is like the Interfacing Arduino with Lora.

Fabricating PCB for LoRa Shield

Since our circuit is prepared, we can continue with structuring our PCB. I opened by PCB plan programming and started shaping my tracks. When the PCB configuration was finished my board looked something like this demonstrated as follows

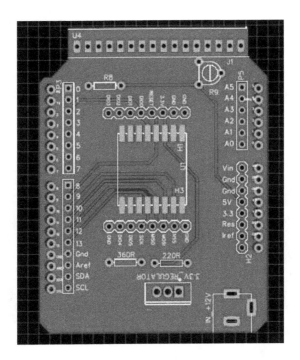

You can likewise download the plan documents in GERBER group and manufacture it to get your sheets.

Presently, that our Design is prepared the time to get them created. To complete the PCB is very simple, essentially pursue the means underneath

Stage 1: Get into www.pcbgogo.com, join if this is your first time. At that point, in the PCB Prototype tab enter the elements of your PCB, the quantity of layers and the quantity of PCB you require. Accepting the PCB is 800mm×800mm you can fix the measurements as demonstrated as follows.

Stage 2: Proceed by tapping on the Quote Now catch. You will be taken to a page where to set couple of extra parameters whenever required like the material utilized track dispersing and so on. Be that as it may, generally the default esteems will work fine. The main thing that we need to consider here is the cost and time. As should be obvious the Construction Time is just two to three days and it costs $5 for our PSB. You would then be able to choose a favored transporting strategy dependent on your prerequisite.

Stage 3: The last advance is to transfer the Gerber record and continue with the installment. To ensure the procedure is smooth PCBGOGO confirms if your Gerber record is substantial before continuing with the installment. Thusly you can sure that your PCB is creation well disposed and will contact you as submitted.

Assembling the PCB

After the board was requested, it contacted me after some days however dispatch in a conveniently named well-stuffed box and like consistently the nature of the PCB was great.

I turned on my fastening bar and began gathering the Board. Since the Footprints, cushions, vias and silkscreen are impeccably of the correct shape and size I had no issue gathering the board. When the fastening was finished the board resembled this beneath, as should be obvious it fits cozy on my Arduino Uno Board.

Since our venture has an Arduino LoRa transmitter and an Arduino LoRa recipient we will require two shields one for collector and the other for transmitter. So I continued with securing another PCB, both the PCB with LoRa module and LCD is demonstrated as follows.

As should be obvious just the beneficiary LoRa shied (left one) has a LCD associated it, the transmitter side just comprises of the LoRa module. We will further associate a GPS module to the transmitter side as examined beneath.

Connecting GPS module to LoRa Transmitter

The GPS module utilized here is the NEO-6M GPS module, the module can work on low power with a little structure factor making it reasonable for following applications. Anyway there are numerous different GPS modules accessible which we have utilized already in various sort of vehicle following and area location applications.

The module works in 5V and conveys utilizing Serial correspondence at 9600 baud rate. Thus we control the module to +5V stick of Arduino and associate the Rx and Tx stick to advanced stick D4 and D3 separately as demonstrated as follows

The pins D4 as well as D3 will be designed as programming sequential pins. When fueled the NEO-6M GPS module will search for satellite association and the will consequently yield all the data sequentially. This yield information will be in the NMEA sentence design which represents NMEA and is the standard configuration for all GPS gadgets. This information will be enormous and most time we need to convey it physically to acquire the ideal outcome. Fortunate for us there is a library called TinyGPS++ which does all the truly difficult work for us. You additionally need to include the LoRa library on the off chance that you have not done it yet. So how about we download both the library from beneath connection

Download TinyGPS++ Arduino Library

Download Arduino LoRa Library

The connection will download a ZIP record which would then be able to be added to the Arduino IDE by following the order Sketch - > Include Library - > Add.ZIP library. When you are prepared with the equipment and library we can continue with Programming our Arduino sheets.

Programming Arduino LoRa as GPS Transmitter

We probably aware that the LoRa is a handset gadget, which means it can both send and get data. Anyway in this GPS tracker venture we will utilize one module as transmitter to peruse the co-ordinate data from GPS and send it, while the other module as a recipient which will get the GPS co-ordinate esteems and print it on the LCD. The program for Transmitter as well as Receiver module can be find at the base. Ensure you have introduced the libraries for GPS module and LoRa module before continuing with the code. In this segment we will take a gander at the transmitter code.

Like consistently we start the program by including the required libraries and pins. Here the SPI and LoRa library is utilized for LoRa correspondence and the TinyGPS++ and SoftwareSerial library is utilized for GPS correspondence. The GPS module in my equipment is associated with stick 3 and 4 and consequently we additionally characterize that as pursues

```
#include <SPI.h>

#include <LoRa.h>

#include <TinyGPS++.h>

#include <SoftwareSerial.h>

// Choose two Arduino pins to use for software serial

int RXPin = 3;

int TXPin = 4;
```

Inside the arrangement work we start the sequential screen and furthermore introduce the product sequential as "gpsSerial" for correspondence with our NEO-6M GPS module. Likewise note that I have utilized 433E6 (433 MHz) as my LoRa working recurrence you may need to transform it dependent on the kind of module you are utilizing.

```
void setup() {

  Serial.begin(9600);

  gpsSerial.begin(9600);

  while (!Serial);

  Serial.println("LoRa Sender");

  if (!LoRa.begin(433E6)) {

    Serial.println("Starting LoRa failed!");

    while (1);

  }

  LoRa.setTxPower(20);
```

```
}
```

Inside the circle work we check in the event that the GPS module is putting out certain information, on the off chance that indeed, at that point we read every information and expression it utilizing the gps.encode work. At that point we check that we have gotten a substantial area information utilizing the gps.location.isValid() work.

```
while (gpsSerial.available() > 0)

   if (gps.encode(gpsSerial.read()))

      if (gps.location.isValid())

   {
```

On the off chance that we have gotten a legitimate area we can, at that point start transmitting the scope and longitude esteems. The capacity gps.location.lat() gives the scope co-ordinate as well as the capacity gps.location.lng() gives the longitude co-ordinate. Since we will print them on the 16*2 LCD we need to make reference to when to crap to second line, thus we utilize the watchword "c" to suggest the beneficiary to print the accompanying data on line 2.

```
LoRa.beginPacket();

  LoRa.print("Lat: ");

  LoRa.print(gps.location.lat(), 6);

  LoRa.print("c");

  LoRa.print("Long: ");

  LoRa.print(gps.location.lng(), 6);

  Serial.println("Sent via LoRa");

  LoRa.endPacket();
```

Programming Arduino LoRa as GPS receiver

The transmitter code is now sending the estimation of scope and longitude co-ordinates, presently the beneficiary needs to peruse these qualities and print on the LCD. Correspondingly here we include the library for LoRa module and LCD show and characterize to which sticks the LCD is associated with and furthermore introduce the LoRa module like previously.

```
#include <SPI.h> //SPI Library

#include <LoRa.h> //LoRa Library


#include <LiquidCrystal.h> //Library for LCD

const int rs = 8, en = 7, d4 = 6, d5 = 5, d6 = 4, d7 = 3; // Mention the pin number for LCD connection

LiquidCrystal lcd(rs, en, d4, d5, d6, d7);//Initialize LCD method

void setup() {

  Serial.begin(9600); //Serial for Debugging

  lcd.begin(16, 2); //Initialise 16*2 LCD

  lcd.print("Arduino LoRa"); //Intro Message line 1
```

```
lcd.setCursor(0, 1);

lcd.print("Receiver");  //Intro Message line 2

delay(2000);

if (!LoRa.begin(433 E6))  { //Operate on 433MHz

 Serial.println("Starting LoRa failed!");

 lcd.print("LoRa  Failed");

 while (1);

 }

}
```

Inside the circle work we tune in for information parcels structure the transmitter LoRa module and its size utilizing the LoRa.parsePacket() capacity and store it in "packetSize" variable. In the event that bundles are gotten, at that point we continue with understanding them as characters and print them on the LCD. The program likewise checks in the event that the LoRa module is sending the catchphrase "c", in the event that indeed, at that point prints the rest of the data on the subsequent line.

```
if (packetSize) {    // If packet received

  Serial.print("Received packet '");

  lcd.clear();

  while (LoRa.available()) {

    char incoming = (char)LoRa.read();

    if (incoming == 'c')

    {

      lcd.setCursor(0, 1);

    }

    else

    {
```

```
    lcd.print(incoming);


    }


    }
```

Arduino LoRa GPS Tracker Working

When the equipment and program is prepared we can transfer both the codes in the particular Arduino modules and power them utilizing a 12V connector or USB link. At the point when the Transmitter is fueled you can see the blue LED on the GPS module flickering, this shows the module is searching for satellite association with get co-ordinates. In the interim the Receiver module resolve on and show an appreciated message on the LCD screen. When the transmitter sends the data the recipient module will show it on its LCD as demonstrated as follows

Presently you can move around with the transmitter GPS module and you will see the recipient refreshing its area. To know where precisely the transmitter module is you can peruse the scope and longitude esteems showed on the LCD and enter it into Google maps to get the area on guide as demonstrated as follows.

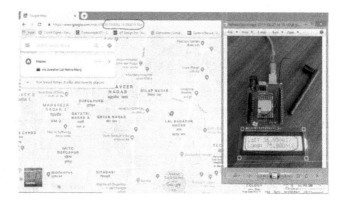

Expectation you comprehended the instructional exercise and delighted in structure something helpful with it.

Code

Lora Sender Code

```
#include <SPI.h>
#include <LoRa.h>
#include <TinyGPS++.h>
#include <SoftwareSerial.h>

// Choose two Arduino pins to use for software serial
int RXPin = 3;
int TXPin = 4;

// Create a TinyGPS++ object
TinyGPSPlus gps;
```

```
SoftwareSerial gpsSerial(RXPin, TXPin);
void setup() {
  Serial.begin(9600);
   gpsSerial.begin(9600);
   while (!Serial);
Serial.println("LoRa Sender");
if (!LoRa.begin(433E6)) {
   Serial.println("Starting LoRa failed!");
   while (1);
 }
LoRa.setTxPower(20);

}
void loop() {

while (gpsSerial.available() > 0)
  if (gps.encode(gpsSerial.read()))

    if (gps.location.isValid())
{
  Serial.println("Sending to LoRa");
  LoRa.beginPacket();
  LoRa.print("Lat: ");
  LoRa.print(gps.location.lat(), 6);
```

```
LoRa.print("c");
LoRa.print("Long: ");
LoRa.print(gps.location.lng(), 6);
Serial.println("Sent via LoRa");
LoRa.endPacket();
}
}
```

Lora Receiver Code

```
/*Program to receive the value of temperature and
Humidity via LoRa and prin on LCD
 *
 */
#include <SPI.h> //SPI Library
#include <LoRa.h> //LoRa Library
#include <LiquidCrystal.h> //Library for LCD
const int rs = 8, en = 7, d4 = 6, d5 = 5, d6 = 4, d7 = 3;
//Mention the pin number for LCD connection
LiquidCrystal lcd(rs, en, d4, d5, d6, d7);//Initialize LCD
method
void setup() {
  Serial.begin(9600); //Serial for Debugging
```

```
lcd.begin(16, 2); //Initialise 16*2 LCD
lcd.print("Arduino LoRa"); //Intro Message line 1
lcd.setCursor(0, 1);
lcd.print("Receiver"); //Intro Message line 2
delay(2000);

if (!LoRa.begin(433E6))  { //Operate on 433MHz
  Serial.println("Starting  LoRa  failed!");
  lcd.print("LoRa  Failed");
  while  (1);
 }
}
void loop() {
int packetSize  = LoRa.parsePacket();

 if (packetSize)  {     // If packet received
  Serial.print("Received  packet '");
  lcd.clear();
while  (LoRa.available())  {
    char incoming  = (char)LoRa.read();
    if (incoming  == 'c')
    {
      lcd.setCursor(0, 1);
    }
```

```
    else
    {
      lcd.print(incoming);
    }


  }
}
}
```

7.How to install Node-RED on Raspberry Pi to Control an LED

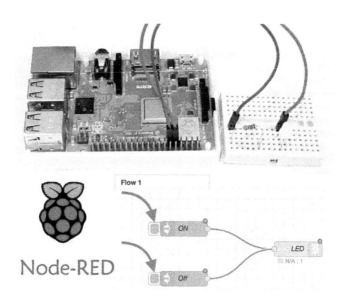

Ever thought about whether there was an approach to make basic models of IoT arrangements without going through days composing codes or to assemble functional propelled ventures without coding. Truly, this is conceivable with the Node-Red Platform. Created by IBM, Node-RED is a open-source programming instrument for wiring together equipment gadgets, APIs and online administrations in new and intriguing way. It gives a program based administrator that makes it easy to wire together 'streams' utilizing the wide scope of hubs in the palette that can be conveyed to its runtime in a solitary snap.

Hub RED is an incredible asset for structure (IoT) applications with the objective of improving the programming part.

It utilizes visual programming allows you to interface code squares, known as hubs, together to play out an errand. For the present instructional exercise, we will look convey basic ventures on the raspberry pi utilizing Node-RED. The raspberry pi hub red instructional exercise will cover;

1.   Introducing Node-RED on the Raspberry Pi.

2.   Prologue to the Node-RED UI

3.   The most effective method to set up Node-RED streams

4.   The most effective method to control Raspberry Pi GPIO pins with Node-RED

5. The most effective method to utilize Node-RED sources of info, yields and if-else like basic leadership utilizing switches

Pre-requisites

This will be founded on the Raspbian extend OS and I will expect you know to frame the Raspberry Pi with it, and you know how to SSH into the Pi utilizing a terminal programming like putty. In the event that you have issues with any of this, there are huge amounts of Raspberry Pi Tutorials on this site can help.

To effectively finish the instructional exercise, I will educate you make use with respect to a screen associated with the raspberry pi or you utilize the VNC Viewer programming. On the off chance that you don't have a Monitor and beginning crisp with Pi you can peruse this Headless Raspberry Pi set-up to continue with this instructional exercise. While Node-Red keeps running from an internet browser and can be gotten to on your PC to which the Pi is associated by means of the Pi's IP address, I accept the VNC/screen experience will give you a superior hang of things.

As a demo to demonstrate how Node-Red functions, we will utilize Node-RED to program the Raspberry Pi to control a LED associated with its GPIO and later alter the program to enable the LED to be controlled from a material pushbutton associated with the Pi's GPIO.

Required Components

The accompanying segments are required to fabricate this task;

1. Raspberry Pi 3 with SD card preloaded with Raspbian Stretch Preloaded
2. 100 ohms resistor (1)
3. LED (1)
4. Breadboard (1)
5. Male-to-female jumper wires
6. Tactile push button (1)

Installing Node-RED on Raspberry Pi

While Node-Red comes preinstalled on the Raspbian Stretch OS, we have to update it before we can appreciate a portion of its most recent highlights. Overhauling the Node-Red will

Overhaul the current client to LTS 8.x or 10.x Node.js and most recent Node-RED

Relocate any current universally introduced hubs into the clients ~/.hub red space so they can be overseen by means of the palette director, it DOES NOT refresh any client introduced existing hubs. This must be done physically by the client (see underneath).

Alternatively (re)install the additional hubs that are pre-introduced on a full Raspbian Pi picture.

Notwithstanding, the way toward updating the Node-Red is like introducing another one so for this instructional exercise we will simply treat it like another establishment so individuals utilizing different OS renditions can pursue.

Pursue the means underneath to Install/Upgrade Node-RED on your Raspberry Pi.

We begin by redesigning and refreshing the pi, to guarantee everything on it is exceptional and dodge similarity issues. Do this by opening a terminal or by means of ssh, and run;

Sudo apt-get update

followed by

sudo apt-get upgrade

With this done, run the slam content beneath on the terminal;

bash <(curl -sL https://raw.githubusercontent.com/node-red/raspbian-deb-package/master/resources/update-nodejs-and-NodeRed)

The slam content will do the accompanying things

1. Inquire as to whether you need to (re)install the additional Pi hubs

2. Spare a rundown of any universally introduced hub red-hubs found in/usr/lib/node_modules

3. adept get evacuate existing Node-Red

4. expel any hub red pairs from/usr/canister and/usr/neighborhood/container

5. Expel any hub red modules from/usr/lib/node_modules and/usr/neighborhood/lib/node_modules

6. Identify if Node.js was introduced from Node.js bundle or Debian

7. If not v8 or more up to date - expel as fitting and introduce most recent v8 or v10 LTS (not utilizing adept).

8. Get out npm reserve and .hub cheat store to expel any past adaptations of the code

9. Introduce Node-RED most recent form

10. Re-introduce under the client account any hubs that had recently been introduced universally

11. Re-introduce the additional Pi hubs whenever required

12. Revamp all hubs - to recompile any doubles to coordinate most recent Node.js adaptation

13. Include hub red-begin, hub red-stop and hub red-log directions to/usr/canister

14. Include menu alternate route and symbol

15. Include framework content and set client

16. In the event that on a Pi include a CPU temperature - > IoT model

The slam content above runs numerous directions as sudo and deletes existing Node.js and the center Node-RED registries. You can check the substance of the content on this GitHub page before running it to make sure it won't influence any undertaking you as of now have on the Pi.

With the establishment is finished you must observe the Node-Red symbol under the programming applications rundown of your menu.

Launching Node-RED in Raspberry Pi

Hub Red can be propelled through the menu area from your raspberry pi's work area, by means of the terminal, or over ssh.

To dispatch on the raspberry pi's work area, Click on the Raspberry symbol, float your mouse on Programming click on Node-RED (Menu>Programming>NodeRed) to dispatch it.

It can likewise be propelled from ssh or terminal by running;

```
node-red-start
```

```
Start Node-RED

Once Node-RED has started, point a browser at http://192.168.0.16:1880
On Pi Node-RED works better with the Firefox browser

Use    node-red-stop                              to stop Node-RED
Use    node-red-start                             to start Node-RED again
Use    node-red-log                               to view the recent log output
Use    sudo systemctl enable nodered.service      to autostart Node-RED at every
Use    sudo systemctl disable nodered.service to disable autostart on boot

To find more nodes and example flows - go to http://flows.nodered.org
You may also need to install and upgrade npm
       sudo apt-get install npm
       sudo npm i -g npm@2.x
```

You should see a window like the one beneath indicating hub red dispatch on the work area.

When you see this, go to menu->internet and dispatch the chromium internet browser. While your Raspberry pi does not require the web to run Node-Red, it utilizes a program as its interface.

With chromium propelled enter localhost:1880 in the location bar pursued by the enter key. 1880 is the port on the raspberry pi on which Node-Red is preset to convey. This should show the Node-Red interface as appeared in the picture underneath.

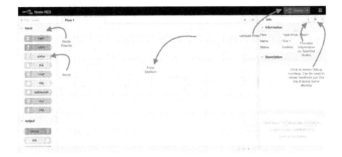

Understanding the Node-RED interface

The Node-Red interface includes the stream board, the hubs palette, the investigate support and the data comfort as featured in the picture above.

The stream board is the place the hubs are consolidated to make a program which in Node-Red is called stream, while the Node palette includes objects which are illustrative of equipment, conventions and programming highlights related with gadgets. It incorporates conventions like MQTT for IoT, and GPIO yield and info modes for sheets like the raspberry pi. The data comfort gives data on featured/chose objects while the investigate support works simply like the Arduino Serial screen and can give criticism while the stream is running. The send catch is utilized to transfer the stream to target equipment. Menu catch contains distinctive transfer types to enable you to get the best out of your task. With Node-Red ready for action, we would now be able to continue to assemble the demo venture.

Schematics

As referenced during the presentation, our demo venture for now will be to control the Raspberry Pi's GPIO utilizing a Node-RED stream. To demonstrate the variety in the GPIO's state, we will associate a LED to the GPIO to such an extent that when that specific GPIO stick is turned on, the LED goes ahead and the other way around.

Associate the LED to the Raspberry PI as appeared in the schematics underneath.

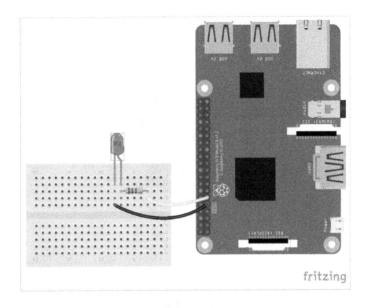

I likewise fabricate the equivalent on my equipment utilizing a breadboard, LED, resistor and some associating wires. My equipment set-up looks something like this once the associations are made.

This task can be effectively changed over into a Home computerization venture, just by supplanting the LED with a transfer and any AC machine, figure out how to do that by experiencing different Home Automation Projects.

Creating a Flow in Node-RED

With the LED associated, we can carry on to build up the stream. Projects in NodeRed are called streams simply like the Arduino IDE calls them outlines. Streams are made utilizing a mix of hubs. You can make different streams which would all be able to keep running simultaneously, yet for this instructional exercise, we will make a solitary stream to turn the LED on/off.

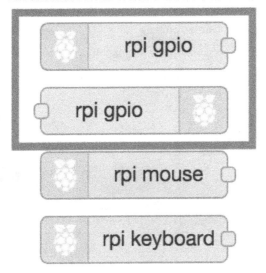

To start, Scroll to the base of the Nodes palette, you will see the raspberry pi hubs segment towards the end with two hubs named rpigpio. These hubs are utilized for speaking with the raspberry pi's GPIO. One of the Nodes is for info while the other is for yield separated by the situation of the raspberry pi's logo. For the information hub, the logo precedes the content, while for yield hub the logo comes after the content as appeared in the picture underneath.

For this instructional exercise we will utilize the yield hub, drag it into the stream area of the interface. This progression is like proclaiming a specific stick of your Arduino as Output utilizing the pinMode() order. Double tap on the Output hub and a spring up window will open as appeared beneath to permit you alter the properties of the hub.

Under the stick property area, select GPIO17 (stick 11). At that point set the sort property to "advanced Output" and tick the "Introduce stick state?" check box leaving the "underlying degree of stick" alternative as low (0). Give the hub whatever name you like and snap the done catch.

The name of the hub ought to naturally change to the one you entered under the properties setting. For instance I named it as LED and henceforth the hub name is additionally changed as LED as demonstrated as follows.

To turn the LED on/off, we have to utilize an information, something to drive the activity. While we could utilize a push catch, I need to utilize this to present the element in Node-RED that permits the infusion of messages into streams. These element is known as the infuse Node. We will utilize two infuse hubs. One will be to turn the LED on while the other will be to turn it off.

Go to the hub palette and drag the infuse hub to the stream. It's the principal hub in the palette with a bolt, the infuse hub is featured in the picture beneath.

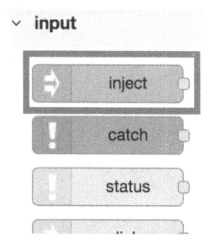

Double tap on it to alter its properties. Change the information type to string by tapping the dropdown before payload, and Enter 1 in the Payload box. The incentive in the payload box is the thing that will be infused into the stream when the hub is squeezed. Set the name of hub to "ON" Press the "Done" catch to spare.

Rehash the above for the subsequent hub, setting the payload incentive to "0" and its name as "off" as demonstrated as follows.

Under the properties work, the rehash dropdown can be utilized to robotize the infusion so the catches are squeezed at interims. This can be utilized to make the flicker impact. Combine the hubs as demonstrated as follows, by hauling the dark dab on one of the hubs to the next to make the stream.

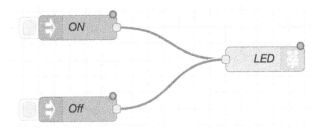

With that done, we have now finished our absolute first Node-Red Flow.

Subsequent stage is for us to convey the stream on the raspberry pi. Snap the red convey catch. You should see "effectively sent" streak at the highest point of the screen as demonstrated as follows.

Successfully deployed

Snap the dark catch behind the infuse hubs to actuate every one of the hubs.

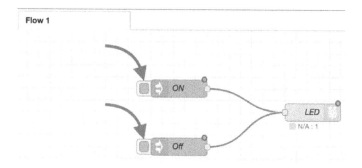

By tapping on the "on" infuse hub, you should see effectively infused "on" showed and the LED please. The LED ought to go off when the "off" infuse hub is clicked.

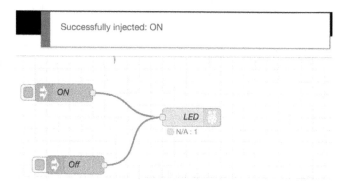

Adding a Pushbutton/Switch in Node-RED interface with Raspberry Pi

To disclose how to associate/add an info component to your stream, we will take the above stream further by adding a pushbutton to supplant the infuse hubs.

Associate the pushbutton to the raspberry pi, with the end goal that, one leg of the pushbutton is associated with ground and the other is associated with GPIO stick 4(pin 11) of the raspbery pi, as appeared in the schematics beneath.

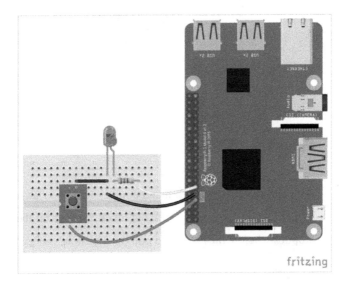

With this done, Go back to Node-Red and erase the two infuse hubs we utilized before, by tapping on the hubs and squeezing erase on your console or double tapping the hubs and squeezing erase on the spring up window. With that done, look down the hub palette to the raspberry pi area and select the information hub. It is the one with the raspberry pi symbol on the left, before the hub's name.

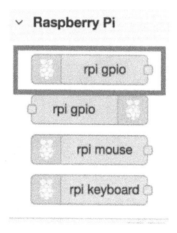

Drag the hub into the stream and double tap on it to alter properties. Set the stick to GPIO 4 (stick 11) and set the dropdown before the resistor to pull-up. This will "pull up"

GPIO 4 to HIGH. Snap on the done catch in the wake of setting the properties.

To permit us settle on sensible choices when the switch is squeezed instead of simply shorting GPIO4 to ground, we will utilize the switch hub. Quest for it in the hub palette, under the capacity segment and drag to the stream.

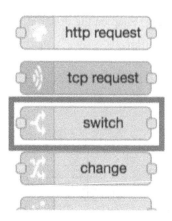

The switch hub permits you settle on choices in a manner like the "if" explanations. It may be set up to have various yields relying upon the information esteem. For this instructional exercise, we will design it with two yield way, to such an extent that, when the msg.payload property is equivalent to 1 (switch isn't squeezed) it ought to pursue the principal way and a subsequent way will be pursued if some other info other than 1 is seen at the input(switch is squeezed). Ways are included utilizing the "+add" catch. Double tap on the hub and design as depicted previously. Snap done when wrapped up.

When you hit the done catch, you should see the two ways reflect in the standpoint of the switch hub, as it will currently have two intersections at the yield.

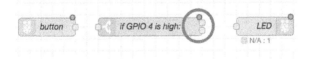

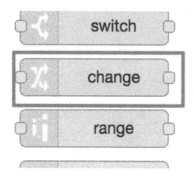

We will utilize two of the change hubs. The payload of the first will be set to 0 as appeared in the picture underneath and the payload of the subsequent one set to one. Snap done subsequent to altering properties for both.

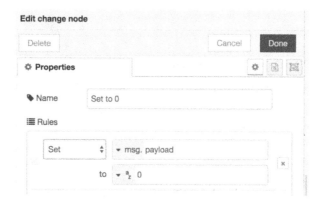

To more readily clarify, recollect that we utilized the draw up resistor? Along these lines, when the catch has not been squeezed, the yield at that stick will be HIGH(1), which means on the off chance that we go it through the switch hub, The LED will be "on", since this ought not be thus, we will utilize the "change" hub to set it as LOW(0). The second "change" hub is utilized to set the incentive to one with the end goal that when something besides the HIGH territory of GPIO stick 4 is recognized, it should turn the LED "on" as this will mean the pushbutton has been squeezed. Interface the change hubs and the remainder of the hubs together as appeared in the picture underneath.

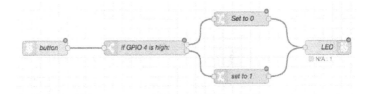

With this done, we are currently prepared to send the task. Go over the association with guarantee everything is as it ought to be, at that point click the send catch. Of course, if fruitful you should see the convey effective popup and now have the option to control the drove utilizing the switch.

While the Node-Red makes it simple and quick to model your work without stressing over the code, it may not really be the best fit, particularly for experienced designers who will need adaptability and authority over the program. In any case, it's an incredible device that permits you model forms in minutes.

Till Next time!

8. MQTT Based Raspberry Pi Home Automation: Controlling Raspberry Pi GPIO using MQTT Cloud

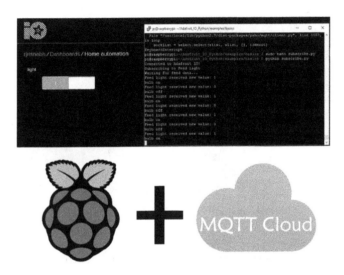

In past instructional exercise we have talked about MQTT Protocol and introduced nearby MQTT server on our Raspberry Pi for controlling the GPIO locally. However, the downside of nearby MQTT server is that we can't control the GPIOs from anyplace on the planet, it just gives benefits locally. Be that as it may, in the event that this MQTT server is facilitated on some cloud, at that point any apparatuses associated with Raspberry Pi can be controlled comprehensively.

Here, in this instructional exercise, we will utilize Adafruit IO as MQTT intermediary to control an AC apparatus associated with Raspberry Pi GPIO. Additionally check other IoT controlled Home Automation instructional exercises:

1. IOT based Voice Controlled Home Automation utilizing ESP8266 and Android App

2. Advanced mobile phone Controlled Home Automation Using Arduino

3. IoT based Web controlled Home Automation utilizing PIC Microcontroller and Adafruit IO

4. IoT based Web Controlled Home Automation utilizing Raspberry Pi

5. Google Assistant Based Voice Controlled Home Automation utilizing DIY Arduino Wi-Fi Shield

Components Required

1. Raspberry Pi with Raspbian Stretch installed in it.
2. Relay Module
3. Bulb
4. Jumper Wires

Here, we will utilize SSH to get to Raspberry Pi on the PC. You can utilize VNC or Remote Desktop association on the PC, or can interface your Raspberry pi with a screen. Become familiar with arranging Raspberry Pi headlessly here without a screen.

Circuit Diagram

Circuit graph for this IoT Controlled Home apparatuses with MQTT cloud and Raspberry Pi is straightforward, simply associate a bulb with hand-off module on GPIO stick 35 of raspberry Pi.

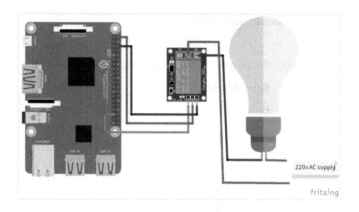

Installing MQTT Cloud Libraries on Raspberry Pi

Here Adafruit IO stage is utilized with Raspberry Pi as MQTT agent. As we have utilized Adafruit IO stage ordinarily in our past instructional exercises likewise we can utilize it in Raspberry Pi.

Simply make a record on Adafruit IO stage and make a feed, in the event that you don't have the foggiest idea how to make feed and redo Adafruit dashboard, at that point pursue the connection.

Following cause dashboard, to introduce couple of libraries in Raspberry Pi to get begin with MQTT.

1. To start with, update Your Pi and Python by issuing following directions

```
sudo apt-get update

sudo apt-get upgrade

sudo pip3 install --upgrade setuptools
```

2. Presently, introduce Rpi.gpio and Adafruit flicker libraries utilizing underneath directions

```
sudo pip3 install RPI.GPIO
```

```
sudo pip3 install adafruit-blinka
```

3. Introduce Adafruit IO library utilizing underneath order

```
sudo pip3 install adafruit-io
```

4. Clone the adafruit models from github utilizing underneath order

```
git                                           clone
https://github.com/adafruit/Adafruit_IO_Python.git
```

5. At that point, explore to the models organizer by entering the accompanying order into the terminal:

```
cd Adafruit_IO_Python/examples/basics
```

In case you don't know which index you're in, you can check this by running pwd.

6. For all models in this organizer, you'll have to set the ADAFRUIT_IO_KEY   and

ADAFRUIT_IO_USERNAME, which can be found from the Adafruit dashboard. As demonstrated as follows

Flip the catch on Adafruit IO dashboard, and you should see the accompanying in the terminal of your Pi.

7. Presently, open the subscribe.py document utilizing nano supervisor. Type following direction to open it

sudo nano subscribe.py

We need to alter this program to control any GPIO from dashboard.

Coding Explanation for controlling Raspberry Pi GPIO with MQTT

To start with, import all the expected libraries to utilize GPIO pins and Adafruit MQTT customer.

```
import RPi.GPIO as GPIO

import sys

from Adafruit_IO import MQTTClient
```

Presently, set GPIO mode and characterize LED stick number and set as yield.

```
GPIO.setmode(GPIO.BOARD)

GPIO.setwarnings(False)

ledPin = 12

GPIO.setup(ledPin, GPIO.OUT)
```

Next, we need to set AIO key and Username that we have found while making the dashboard.

```
ADAFRUIT_IO_KEY = 'YOUR_AIO_KEY'

ADAFRUIT_IO_USERNAME = 'YOUR_AIO_USER
NAME'
```

Enter the feed name that you have given to kill on and the light. Here, it is "light".

```
FEED_ID = 'light'
```

Presently, characterize a capacity that will be called when there will be an occasion occur. In this way, we will buy in the Feed utilizing client.subscribe(FEED_ID)

```
def connected(client):

    client.subscribe(FEED_ID)

    print('Waiting for feed data...')
```

In the wake of buying in the feed, we need to check for the new worth and store it into a payload variable. For this message capacity is called. In this way, at whatever point there is "1" in payload variable, make the drove stick HIGH and for "0" make it LOW.

```python
def message(client, feed_id, payload):

  print('Feed {0} received new value: {1}'.format(feed_i
d, payload))

  if payload == 1:

    GPIO.output(ledPin, GPIO.HIGH)

else:

    GPIO.output(ledPin, GPIO.LOW)
```

Presently, make a MQTT customer to interface with the Adafruit IO stage and send the messages back and forth.

```python
client = MQTTClient(ADAFRUIT_IO_USERNAME,
ADAFRUIT_IO_KEY)

client.on_connect = connected
```

```
client.on_disconnect = disconnected
```

Additionally, take care about legitimate space in the code else it will demonstrate a mistake. Complete python code is given toward the part of the arrangement.

At last, spare the program utilizing ctrl+x and hit the enter. Presently, we need to run the content so as to buy in the messages. So In the terminal sort python subscribe.py and hit the enter.

```
python subscribe.py
```

You will see a message Waiting For Feed Data... as appeared underneath depiction.

Presently, Make sure the transfer module is associated with GPIO stick of Raspberry Pi and after that go to Adafruit IO dashboard and change the light feed. The bulb should turn on when "1" is gotten and killed when "0" is gotten as demonstrated as follows.

Along these lines we can control any machine from anyplace in world by utilizing Raspberry Pi and MQTT cloud

Code

```
import RPi.GPIO as GPIO
import sys
from Adafruit_IO import MQTTClient
GPIO.setmode(GPIO.BOARD)
GPIO.setwarnings(False)
ledPin = 12
GPIO.setup(ledPin, GPIO.OUT)
ADAFRUIT_IO_KEY = 'YOUR_AIO_KEY'
ADAFRUIT_IO_USERNAME =
'YOUR_AIO_USERNAME'
FEED_ID = 'light'
```

```python
def connected(client):
    # Subscribe to changes on a feed named Counter.
    print('Subscribing to Feed {0}'.format(FEED_ID))
    client.subscribe(FEED_ID)
    print('Waiting for feed data...')

def disconnected(client):
    sys.exit(1)

def message(client, feed_id, payload):
    print('Feed {0} received new value: {1}'.format(feed_id, payload))
    if payload == 1:
        GPIO.output(ledPin, GPIO.HIGH)
    else:
        GPIO.output(ledPin, GPIO.LOW)

# Create an MQTT client instance.
client = MQTTClient(ADAFRUIT_IO_USERNAME, ADAFRUIT_IO_KEY)

# Setup the callback functions defined above.
client.on_connect = connected
client.on_disconnect = disconnected
client.on_message = message

# Connect to the Adafruit IO server.
client.connect()
client.loop_blocking()
```

9.Node.js with Arduino: Controlling Brightness of LED through Web Interface

We have seen various instances of Blinking a LED utilizing diverse Microcontrollers and distinctive programming dialects. Today, we will utilize a well known JavaScript system Node.js to control the LED associated with Arduino Uno. We will likewise utilize Node.js to control the brilliance of LED from a site page utilizing Arduino. By few changes and utilizing ESP8266, this can be changed over into an IoT venture where the LED can be controlled from anyplace.

What is Node.js?

The Node.js is a broadly utilized JavaScript-put together system worked with respect to Google Chrome's JavaScript V8 Engine and connected in creating I/O concentrated web applications, for example, single-page applications, video spilling destinations and so forth.

We have completed a useful instructional exercise beforehand on Getting started with Node.js and Raspberry Pi to control a LED. In this instructional exercise, we will pursue the comparable methodology for example the LED will be controlled utilizing two strategies, for example,

Basic LED squint by composing a JavaScript code in the Node.js structure.

Driven Brightness Control Using Node.js structure and a web interface from any program: The Arduino UNO will go about as a webserver and HTML page will be facilitated on a PC or Laptop.

Components Required

Hardware:

1. Arduino UNO Board

2. Driven

3. Resistor

Software:

Arduino IDE: For transferring portrayal to Arduino UNO Board.

Firmata: It is a convention for speaking with various microcontrollers from programming on a PC, cell phone, and so on. The Firmata firmware can be stacked in any microcontroller board (like Arduino, Teensy) and can converse with any workstation, PC or cell phone. Firmata Library accompanies Arduino IDE, so no compelling reason to download from anyplace. We have completed an instructional exercise on controlling Arduino with Raspberry Pi utilizing pyFirmata.

Johnny-Five: Johnny-Five is the JavaScript Based Robotics and IoT stage used to compose codes in JavaScript and Used to make an extension between the Arduino Boards and Computer. Johnny-Five have been tried with an assortment of Arduino-good Boards, for example, Arduino UNO, NANO, Promini, and so on. In this instructional exercise, the Johnny-Five library must be downloaded so as to utilize each one of its highlights. The establishment guide will be clarified later-on in this instructional exercise.

Circuit Diagram

Circuit chart is fundamental, we simply need to interface a LED with Arduino.

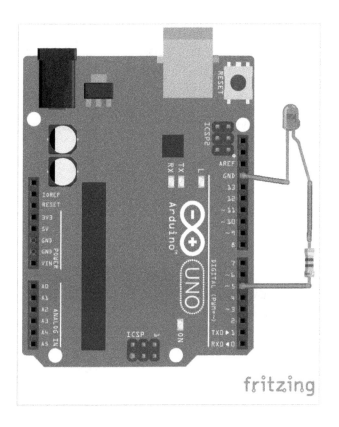

Setting Up Node.js Framework

Prior to beginning the coding and advancement, the Node.js must be downloaded and set up. For downloading the Node.js condition simply pursue straightforward advances.

Stage 1:- Download the .exe record of Node.js from its official site.

Stage 2:- Run the .exe and adhere to the given guidelines in the installer.

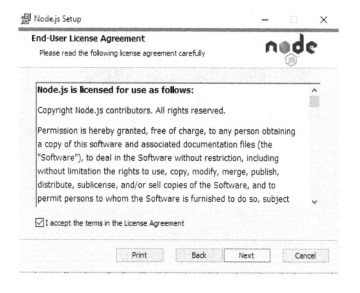

Stage 3:- Restart your PC as it is suggested in the Node.js Document and furthermore to utilize every one of the highlights of Node.js

Stage 4:- To check if the hub has been introduced, open Command Prompt and type Node – v

```
Command Prompt

Microsoft Windows [Version 10.0.17134.706]
(c) 2018 Microsoft Corporation. All rights reserved.

C:\Users\st>Node -v
v10.15.3

C:\Users\st>
```

Stage 5:- The Node.js variant will be shown demonstrating the Node.js is introduced.

Installing Johnny-Five Library

Presently subsequent to downloading the Node.js, make another Folder named "LED_Control" in Documents to keep all the undertaking records in a single spot. Each undertaking document will be kept in the "LED_Control" organizer. Presently download the Johnny-Five Library in the "LED_Control" organizer. To download, pursue ventures beneath:

Stage 1:- Open Command Prompt

Stage 2:- Go to "LED_Control" Folder by following 'cd' direction.

Stage 3:- Run the Command 'npm introduce johnny-five'

```
C:\Users\st\Documents>cd LED_Control

C:\Users\st\Documents\LED_Control>npm install johnny-five

> serialport@6.0.5 install C:\Users\          st\Documents\LED_Control\node_mod
> prebuild-install || node-gyp rebuild

prebuild-install WARN install No prebuilt binaries found (target=10.15.3 runtime=

C:\Users\          st\Documents\LED_Control\node_modules\johnny-five\node_modul
 Files\nodejs\node_modules\npm\node_modules\npm-lifecycle\node-gyp-bin\\..\..\no
 _modules\npm\node_modules\node-gyp\bin\node-gyp.js" rebuild )
Warning: unrecognized setting VCCLCompilerTool/MultiProcessorCompilation
Warning: unrecognized setting VCCLCompilerTool/MultiProcessorCompilation
Building the projects in this solution one at a time. To enable parallel build, p
MSBUILD : error MSB3428: Could not load the Visual C++ component "VCBuild.exe".
ork 2.0 SDK, 2) install Microsoft Visual Studio 2005 or 3) add the location of th
s installed elsewhere. [C:\Users\          st\Documents\LED_Control\node_modul
de_modules\serialport\build\binding.sln]
gyp ERR! build error
gyp ERR! stack Error: `C:\Program Files (x86)\MSBuild\14.0\bin\msbuild.exe` faile
gyp ERR! stack     at ChildProcess.onExit (C:\Program Files\nodejs\node_modules\n
gyp ERR! stack     at ChildProcess.emit (events.js:189:13)
gyp ERR! stack     at Process.ChildProcess._handle.onexit (internal/child_process
gyp ERR! System Windows_NT 10.0.17134
gyp ERR! command "C:\\Program Files\\nodejs\\node.exe" "C:\\Program Files\\nodejs
gyp ERR! cwd C:\Users\          st\Documents\LED_Control\node_modules\johnny-fi
gyp ERR! node -v v10.15.3
gyp ERR! node-gyp -v v3.8.0
gyp ERR! not ok
npm WARN saveError ENOENT: no such file or directory, open 'C:\Users\
npm WARN enoent ENOENT: no such file or directory, open 'C:\Users\          st\
npm WARN LED_Control No description
npm WARN LED_Control No repository field.
npm WARN LED_Control No README data
npm WARN LED_Control No license field.
npm WARN optional SKIPPING OPTIONAL DEPENDENCY: serialport@6.0.5 (node_modules\jo
npm WARN optional SKIPPING OPTIONAL DEPENDENCY: serialport@6.0.5 install: `prebui
npm WARN optional SKIPPING OPTIONAL DEPENDENCY: Exit status 1

+ johnny-five@1.0.0
updated 1 package and audited 4678 packages in 35.541s
found 0 vulnerabilities

C:\Users\st\Documents\LED_Control>
```

Stage 4:- This will introduce all conditions of Johnny-Five.

Stage 5:- Also introduce important libraries utilized in this instructional exercise for controlling splendor of LED. There were 3 libraries utilized here:

express: HTTP server wrapper

socket.io: WebSockets library

serialport: Serial port wrapper

Stage 5:- Run the beneath directions individually to introduce these three libraries.

```
npm install express

npm install socket.io

npm install serialport
```

```
Command Prompt                                    —    □    ×
updated 1 package and audited 4678 packages in 35.541s
found 0 vulnerabilities


C:\Users\st\Documents\LED_Control>npm install express

> serialport@6.0.5 install C:\Users\          st\Documents\LED_Con
> prebuild-install || node-gyp rebuild

prebuild-install WARN install No prebuilt binaries found (target=10

C:\Users\          st\Documents\LED_Control\node_modules\johnny-f
 Files\nodejs\node_modules\npm\node_modules\npm-lifecycle\node-gyp-
 _modules\npm\node_modules\node-gyp\bin\node-gyp.js" rebuild )
Warning: unrecognized setting VCCLCompilerTool/MultiProcessorCompil
Warning: unrecognized setting VCCLCompilerTool/MultiProcessorCompil
Building the projects in this solution one at a time. To enable par
MSBUILD : error MSB3428: Could not load the Visual C++ component "V
2005 or 3) add the location of the component to the system path if
node_modules\firmata\node_modules\serialport\build\binding.sln]
gyp ERR! build error
gyp ERR! stack Error: `C:\Program Files (x86)\MSBuild\14.0\bin\msbu
gyp ERR! stack     at ChildProcess.onExit (C:\Program Files\nodejs\
gyp ERR! stack     at ChildProcess.emit (events.js:189:13)
gyp ERR! stack     at Process.ChildProcess._handle.onexit (internal
gyp ERR! System Windows_NT 10.0.17134
gyp ERR! command "C:\\Program Files\\nodejs\\node.exe" "C:\\Program
gyp ERR! cwd C:\Users\          st\Documents\LED_Control\node_mod
gyp ERR! node -v v10.15.3
gyp ERR! node-gyp -v v3.8.0
gyp ERR! not ok
npm WARN saveError ENOENT: no such file or directory, open 'C:\Users
npm WARN enoent ENOENT: no such file or directory, open 'C:\Users\C
npm WARN LED_Control No description
npm WARN LED_Control No repository field.
npm WARN LED_Control No README data
npm WARN LED_Control No license field.
npm WARN optional SKIPPING OPTIONAL DEPENDENCY: serialport@6.0.5 (n
npm WARN optional SKIPPING OPTIONAL DEPENDENCY: serialport@6.0.5 in
npm WARN optional SKIPPING OPTIONAL DEPENDENCY: Exit status 1

+ express@4.16.4
updated 1 package and audited 4678 packages in 10.49s
found 0 vulnerabilities
```

```
Command Prompt                                    —    □    ×

found 0 vulnerabilities

C:\Users\st\Documents\LED_Control>npm install socket.io

> serialport@6.0.5 install C:\Users\        st\Documents\LED_Control\n
> prebuild-install || node-gyp rebuild

prebuild-install WARN install No prebuilt binaries found (target=10.15.3 r

C:\Users\          st\Documents\LED_Control\node_modules\johnny-five\nod
 Files\nodejs\node_modules\npm\node_modules\npm-lifecycle\node-gyp-bin\\..
_modules\npm\node_modules\node-gyp\bin\node-gyp.js" rebuild )
Warning: unrecognized setting VCCLCompilerTool/MultiProcessorCompilation
Warning: unrecognized setting VCCLCompilerTool/MultiProcessorCompilation
Building the projects in this solution one at a time. To enable parallel b
MSBUILD : error MSB3428: Could not load the Visual C++ component "VCBuild.
2005 or 3) add the location of the component to the system path if it is i
node_modules\firmata\node_modules\serialport\build\binding.sln]
gyp ERR! build error
gyp ERR! stack Error: `C:\Program Files (x86)\MSBuild\14.0\bin\msbuild.exe
gyp ERR! stack     at ChildProcess.onExit (C:\Program Files\nodejs\node_mo
gyp ERR! stack     at ChildProcess.emit (events.js:189:13)
gyp ERR! stack     at Process.ChildProcess._handle.onexit (internal/child_
gyp ERR! System Windows_NT 10.0.17134
gyp ERR! command "C:\\Program Files\\nodejs\\node.exe" "C:\\Program Files\
gyp ERR! cwd C:\Users\         st\Documents\LED_Control\node_modules\jo
gyp ERR! node -v v10.15.3
gyp ERR! node-gyp -v v3.8.0
gyp ERR! not ok
npm WARN saveError ENOENT: no such file or directory, open 'C:\Users\
npm WARN enoent ENOENT: no such file or directory, open 'C:\Users\
npm WARN LED_Control No description
npm WARN LED_Control No repository field.
npm WARN LED_Control No README data
npm WARN LED_Control No license field.
npm WARN optional SKIPPING OPTIONAL DEPENDENCY: serialport@6.0.5 (node_mod
npm WARN optional SKIPPING OPTIONAL DEPENDENCY: serialport@6.0.5 install:
npm WARN optional SKIPPING OPTIONAL DEPENDENCY: Exit status 1

+ socket.io@2.2.0
updated 1 package and audited 4678 packages in 15.943s
found 0 vulnerabilities

C:\Users\Circuit Digest\Documents\LED_Control>
```

```
Command Prompt                                        —    □    ×
found 0 vulnerabilities

C:\Users\st\Documents\LED_Control>npm install serialport

> serialport@6.0.5 install C:\Users\            st\Documents\LED_Control\r
> prebuild-install || node-gyp rebuild

prebuild-install WARN install No prebuilt binaries found (target=10.15.3

C:\Users\            st\Documents\LED_Control\node_modules\johnny-five\nod
Files\nodejs\node_modules\npm\node_modules\npm-lifecycle\node-gyp-bin\\.
_modules\npm\node_modules\node-gyp\bin\node-gyp.js" rebuild )
Warning: unrecognized setting VCCLCompilerTool/MultiProcessorCompilation
Warning: unrecognized setting VCCLCompilerTool/MultiProcessorCompilation
Building the projects in this solution one at a time. To enable parallel
MSBUILD : error MSB3428: Could not load the Visual C++ component "VCBuild
2005 or 3) add the location of the component to the system path if it is
node_modules\firmata\node_modules\serialport\build\binding.sln]
gyp ERR! build error
gyp ERR! stack Error: `C:\Program Files (x86)\MSBuild\14.0\bin\msbuild.exe
gyp ERR! stack     at ChildProcess.onExit (C:\Program Files\nodejs\node_mo
gyp ERR! stack     at ChildProcess.emit (events.js:189:13)
gyp ERR! stack     at Process.ChildProcess._handle.onexit (internal/child
gyp ERR! System Windows_NT 10.0.17134
gyp ERR! command "C:\\Program Files\\nodejs\\node.exe" "C:\\Program Files\
gyp ERR! cwd C:\Users\            st\Documents\LED_Control\node_modules\jc
gyp ERR! node -v v10.15.3
gyp ERR! node-gyp -v v3.8.0
gyp ERR! not ok
npm WARN saveError ENOENT: no such file or directory, open 'C:\Users\Circu
npm WARN enoent ENOENT: no such file or directory, open 'C:\Users\Circuit
npm WARN LED_Control No description
npm WARN LED_Control No repository field.
npm WARN LED_Control No README data
npm WARN LED_Control No license field.
npm WARN optional SKIPPING OPTIONAL DEPENDENCY: serialport@6.0.5 (node_mod
npm WARN optional SKIPPING OPTIONAL DEPENDENCY: serialport@6.0.5 install:
npm WARN optional SKIPPING OPTIONAL DEPENDENCY: Exit status 1

+ serialport@7.1.4
updated 1 package and audited 4678 packages in 11.053s
found 0 vulnerabilities

C:\Users\st\Documents\LED_Control>
```

As told before the venture is partitioned in two sections:

1. Right off the bat, Arduino Blinking LED with Node.js

2. Also, Controlling LED Brightness from web interface utilizing Arduino and Node.js.

Blinking LED with Arduino and Node.js

To flicker LED, the Arduino must be Set up to speak with Computer.

Setting up Arduino UNO for Blinking LED:

So as to make Arduino UNO acknowledge direction from Laptop to Control LED, the Firmata firmware must be stacked in to the Arduino UNO. **To stack the Firmata Firmware**, simply pursue these straightforward advances:

1. **Interface** the Arduino UNO utilizing USB link

2. **Open** Arduino IDE and click Arduino UNO board (If utilizing other board at that point select separate one) from Tools.

3. **Select** the Respective COM port of associated Arduino UNO

4. Presently discover the Firmata Sketch utilizing **Menu - > File - > Examples - > Firmata - > StandardFirmata.**

5. Transfer the **"StandardFirmata"** sketch by going to File - > Upload.

This will stack the Firmata Sketch onto Arduino UNO and now the Arduino UNO is prepared to acknowledge any order from PC.

Composing Node.js program for Blinking LED:

To compose a Node.js program open any word processor (Notepad, Notepad++, and so forth.) and glue the **'blink_led'** code appended toward the part of the arrangement and spare it with an expansion of '.js' for example **(blink_led.js)** in the **"LED_Control"** envelope made previously. We will talk about significant strides in **blink_led.js** code record.

At first characterize the Pin of microcontroller where driven is associated. In this model, the LED is associated with Pin 5 of Arduino UNO. The 'var' in Node.js speaks to variable revelation.

```
var led_pin=5;
```

The **johnny-five** module should be incorporated and the board should be chosen. The modules in Node.js are libraries. The capacity **'require()'** will get to the module.

```
var johnny_five=require("johnny-five");

var arduino_board=new johnny_five.Board();
```

The **console.log** proclamation is like print articulation and it will print message. What's more, the LED stick is set to yield mode and the characterized deferral is given to squint drove.

```
console.log("LED has Started Blinking!");

var led = new johnny_five.Led(led_pin);

led.blink(100);
```

Presently to run the program pursue ventures beneath:

1. Open Command Prompt

2. Find **"LED_Control"** envelope by following 'disc' direction

3. Run **'Hub led_blink.js'** direction. In the event that effectively executed it will **demonstrate "Drove has Started Blinking!"** as appeared in the picture beneath.

```
Command Prompt - Node blink_led.js

C:\Users\st\Documents\LED_Control>Node blink_led.js
1556017678734 Available COM4
1556017678757 Connected COM4
1556017682543 Repl Initialized
>> LED has Started Blinking!
>>
```

4. The drove will begin flickering in the Arduino UNO Pin 5.

5. Also, this completes the initial segment of our instructional exercise for example **Squinting LED with Node.js**

Controlling LED Brightness using Arduino and Node.js Webserver

Like **Blinking a LED with Node.js,** this segment will likewise have a few sections for example Setting up Arduino UNO, Setting up Web Interface and Writing a Node.js program.

Setting up Arduino UNO to control Brightness of LED:

To set up the Arduino UNO, essentially transfer the sketch "arduino_control.ino" into Arduino UNO board and that's it. This will set the Arduino Board and you can download the total code with HTML documents. The "arduino_control.ino" code has following significant advances included.

At first the baud rate is set at 9600.

```
Serial.begin(9600);
```

The sequential port consistently searches for approaching byte and the byte is composed to Pin 5 which is a PWM Pin.

```
while(!Serial.available());

analogWrite(5, Serial.read());
```

That is it. This will set the Arduino to hook the byte to **PWM** stick and will change the splendor of LED.

Setting up Web Interface:

To control the brilliance of drove utilizing web interface, one little bit of **HTML code** is composed to **have an interface in the Browser**. To have interface pursue basic strides beneath:

1. Make another organizer named **"public"** inside the **"LED_Control"** envelope made previously.

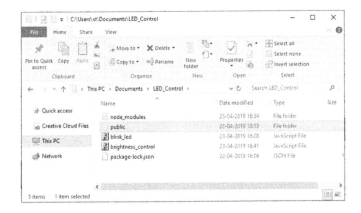

2. Presently download the **"index.html"** and **"style.css"** documents and move the two records inside **"general society"** envelope made in initial step above.

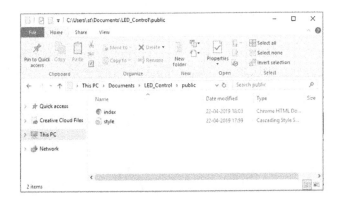

This will make a **slider on page** to control the brilliance of LED utilizing Node.js as well as Arduino.

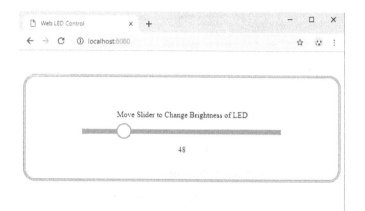

Controlling a LED from page is intriguing to learn and it can finished with other microcontroller by making a webserver and host the website page on webserver.

Composing Node.js program to control Brightness of LED:

Subsequent stage would compose the **"brightness_control.js"** sketch utilizing Node.js and executing the code. The execution of the code will be bit like the **Blinking a LED with Node.js.**

To compose a Node.js program open any content manager (Notepad, Notepad++, and so forth.) and glue the **'brightness_control"** code joined toward the part of the arrangement and spare it with an augmentation of **'.js'** for example (**brightness_control.js**) in the **"LED_Control"** organizer made previously. You can likewise download the code from here.

Like Blink Led Node.js program, this area will likewise utilize modules (library). Incorporate the 'express', 'http' and 'sequential port' module.

```
var express = require('express');

app = express();

server = require('http').createServer(app);

io = require('socket.io').listen(server);

var SerialPort = require("serialport")//.SerialPort
```

Presently set the COM port and baudrate. Note that in windows, it will be COM with augmentation of number (COM6, COM4, COM24 and so on.), so set underneath as required after '/'. Likewise set buadrate.

```
var serialPort = new SerialPort("/COM4", { baudRate : 9600 });
```

Begin to listen the server at port 8080.

```
server.listen(8080);
```

Set the splendor at 0 at first. At that point lock the splendor information to IO with attachments module, which is a websocket module. The information will get by Web Interface utilizing attachment convention.

```
io.sockets.on('connection', function (socket) {

socket.on('led', function (data) {

brightness = data.value;
```

```
var buf = new Buffer(1);

buf.writeUInt8(brightness, 0);

serialPort.write(buf);
```

Presently transmit the LED splendor worth got from attachment to LED stick.

```
io.sockets.emit('led', {value: brightness});

});

socket.emit('led', {value: brightness});

});
```

Presently just to investigate, include a print explanation toward the end. Console.log is a print proclamation in Node.js.

```
console.log("Web Server Started go to 'http://localhost :8080' in your Browser.");
```

Presently to run the program by following the means beneath:

1. Open Command Prompt

2. Find **"LED_Control"** envelope by following **'cd'** order

3. Run **'Hub brightness_control.js'** direction. On the off chance that effectively executed it will indicate **"Web Server Started go to "http://localhost:8080" in your Browser."** just underneath the order.

```
Select Command Prompt - Node brightness_control.js

C:\Users\st\Documents\LED Control>Node brightness_control.js
Web Server Started go to 'http://localhost:8080' in your Browser.
(node:12316) [DEP0005] DeprecationWarning: Buffer() is deprecated due to secu
uffer.alloc(), Buffer.allocUnsafe(), or Buffer.from() methods instead.
```

4. Presently go to your program and type "localhost:8080" in the url.

5. To change the splendor simply move the slider from 0-255 qualities.

The total code of both segment is appended underneath.

Code

Part 1 - Node.js Code for LED Blinking:

```
var led_pin=5;
var johnny_five=require("johnny-five");
```

```javascript
var arduino_board=new johnny_five.Board();
arduino_board.on("ready", function() {
  console.log("LED has Started Blinking!");
  var led = new johnny_five.Led(led_pin);
  led.blink(100);
});
```

Part 2 -a- Arduino code for controlling Brightness of LED:

```c
void setup()
{
  Serial.begin(9600);
}
void loop()
{
  while(!Serial.available());   //wait until a byte was received
  analogWrite(5, Serial.read());//output received byte
}
```

Part 2 -b - Node.js Code for Controlling Brightness of LED:

```javascript
var express = require('express');
app = express();
server = require('http').createServer(app);
io = require('socket.io').listen(server);

var SerialPort = require("serialport")//.SerialPort
var serialPort = new SerialPort("/COM4", { baudRate:
9600 });

server.listen(8080);
app.use(express.static('public'));

var brightness = 0;

io.sockets.on('connection', function (socket) {
    socket.on('led', function (data) {
        brightness = data.value;

        var buf = new Buffer(1);
        buf.writeUInt8(brightness, 0);
        serialPort.write(buf);

        io.sockets.emit('led', {value: brightness});
    });
```

```
        socket.emit('led', {value: brightness});
});


console.log("Web Server Started go to
'http://localhost:8080' in your Browser.");
```

10. How to Use Deep Sleep Mode in ESP8266 for Power Saving

Power Saving

As the IoT upset is blasting with each and every day, the quantity of associated gadgets are expanding all around quickly. In future, a big part of the gadgets will be associated together and will impart progressively. One of the issue looked by these gadget is control utilization. This power utilization factor is one of the basic and conclusive factor for any IoT gadget and IoT Projects.

As we realize that ESP8266 is one of the most prevalent module to fabricate any IoT venture, so in this article we find out about sparing force while utilizing ESP8266 in any IoT application. Here we transfer LM35 temperature sensor information to ThingSpeak cloud in 15 seconds interim and during those 15 seconds ESP8266 stays in DeepSleep mode to spare the power

Different Methods to Minimize Power Consumption

There are a few different ways to advance the power utilization in the **installed** and **IoT gadgets**. The improvement should be possible on equipment and programming. Now and again we can't streamline equipment segments to diminish the Power utilization, yet clearly we can do it on programming side by changing and improving code directions and capacities. Not just this, designers can likewise **Modify the Clock Frequency to Reduce Microcontroller Power Consumption.**

We can compose a firmware to make the equipment rest when there is no trade of information and play out the characterized assignment in a specific interim. In resting mode, the associated equipment draws exceptionally less power and thus the battery can keep going long. You can likewise peruse **Minimizing Power Consumption in Microcontrollers**, in case that you need to find out about power utilization procedures.

ESP8266 modules are the most broadly utilized Wi-Fi modules accompanies numerous highlights in little size having various modes including rest mode and these modes can be gotten to utilizing some adjustment in equipment and programming. To get familiar with ESP8266, you can check our **IoT based undertakings utilizing ESP826 Wi-Fi module**, some of them are recorded beneath:

1. **Interfacing ESP8266 NodeMCU with Atmega16 Microcontroller to Send an Email**

2. **Sending Temperature and Humidity sensor information to Firebase Real-Time Database utilizing NodeMCU ESP8266**

3. **IoT Controlled LED utilizing Google Firebase Console and ESP8266 NodeMCU**

Here we will clarify **distinctive rest modes** accessible in ESP8266 and exhibit them by sending temperature information to **Thingspeak server** in an ordinary interim utilizing the **profound rest mode**.

Components Required

1. ESP8266 Wi-Fi Module

2. Jumper wires

3. LM35 temperature sensor

Types of Sleep Modes in ESP8266

Esp8266 module works in the accompanying modes:

1. **Dynamic mode:** In this mode, entire chip is fueled on and chip can get, transmit the information. Clearly, this is the most power expending mode.

2. **Modem-rest mode:** In this mode, the CPU is operational and the Wi-Fi radios are debilitated. This mode can be utilized in the applications which requires the CPU to work, as in **PWM**. It makes the Wi-Fi Modem circuit to mood killer while associated with the Wi-Fi AP (Access Point) without any information transmission to enhance control utilization.

3. **Light-rest mode:** In this mode, the CPU as well as all peripherals are stopped. Any wake-up, for example, outside hinders will awaken the chip.

Without information transmission, the Wi-Fi Modem circuit can be killed and CPU suspended to spare power utilization.

4. **Profound rest mode**: In this mode just the **RTC** is useful and every other part of the chip are fueled off. This mode is helpful where the information is transmitted after quite a while interims.

	Item	Modem-sleep	Light-sleep	Deep-sleep
	Wi-Fi	OFF	OFF	OFF
	System clock	ON	OFF	OFF
	RTC	ON	ON	ON
	CPU	ON	Pending	OFF
	Substrate current	15 mA	0.4 mA	~ 20 µA
Average current	DTIM = 1	16.2 mA	1.8 mA	
	DTIM = 3	15.4 mA	0.9 mA	-
	DTIM = 10	15.2 mA	0.55 mA	

Deep-Sleep Mode in ESP8266

Modem-rest and Light-rest are valuable when you need ESP8266 module working while a portion of the capacities shut down. Be that as it may, in the event that you need some genuine power control, at that point go for the Deep-rest mode. The general normal current is under 1mA. At 2.5V the present prerequisite is just 20 μA.

Steps to use the Deep-sleep mode:

1. Associate the module with the Wi-Fi AP

2. Play out an errand like perusing a sensor esteem, distributing a MQTT message, and so on.

3. Rest for a characterized number of microseconds

4. Rehash the above procedure

Rest time is characterized in microseconds. As per the ESP8266 SDK, you can rest for 4,294,967,295 μs which is about ~71 minutes.

Setting up the ESP8266 Module:

Interface the RST stick of ESP8266 with the GPIO 16 for example D0 stick. **GPIO 16 is significant stick has a WAKE highlight.**

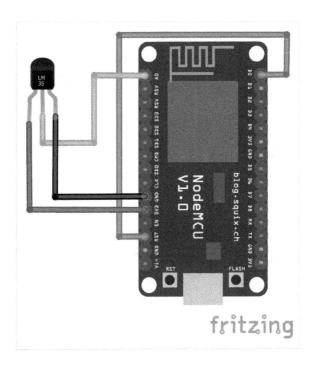

Interface the **LM35 temperature sensor** with the A0 stick
of NodeMCU.

At the point when the ESP module has HIGH on RST stick, it is in running state. When it gets LOW sign on RST stick, the ESP restarts.

Set clock utilizing profound rest mode, when the clock closes then the D0 stick sends the LOW sign to RST stick and the module will wake up by restarting it.

Presently, the equipment is prepared and very much arranged. The temperature readings will be sent on the Thingspeak server. For this, make a record on thingspeak.com and make a channel by experiencing the underneath steps.

Presently, duplicate the Write API key. Which will be utilized in the ESP code.

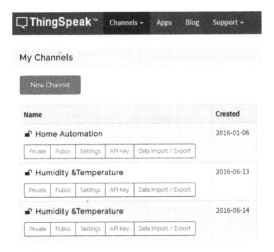

ESP8266 Deep Sleep Mode Programming

The effectively accessible **Arduino IDE will be utilized to program ESP8266 module**. Ensure that all the ESP8266 board records are introduced.

Begin with including all the significant libraries required.

```
#include <ESP8266WiFi.h>
```

When all libraries are incorporated for getting to the capacities at that point allocate the API compose key, design your Wi-Fi name and secret phrase. At that point announce every one of the factors for further use where information to be put away.

```
String apiWritekey = "*************"; // replace with your THINGSPEAK WRITEAPI key here

char ssid[] = "******"; // your wifi SSID name

char password[] = "******"; // wifi pasword
```

Presently, make a capacity to interface the module with Wi-Fi system utilizing wifi.begin() capacity and afterward check persistently till the module isn't associated with Wi-Fi utilizing while circle.

```
void connect1() {

  WiFi.disconnect();

  delay(10);
```

```
WiFi.begin(ssid, password);

while (WiFi.status() != WL_CONNECTED) {
```

Make another capacity to send the information to thingspeak server. Here, a string will be sent which contains the API compose key, field number and information that must be sent. At that point send this string utilizing client.print() work.

```
void data() {

if (client.connect(server,80))

{

  String tsData = apiWritekey;

      tsData +="&field1=";

      tsData += String(tempF);

      tsData += "\r\n\r\n";
```

```
client.print("POST /update HTTP/1.1\n");

client.print("Host: api.thingspeak.com\n");
```

Call the connect1 work which will call the capacity to interface Wi-Fi then take the readings of the temperature and convert it into Celsius.

```
void setup() {

  Serial.begin(115200);

  Serial.println("device is in Wake up mode");

  connect1();

  int value = analogRead(A0);

  float volts=(value/1024.0)*5.0;

  tempC = volts*100.0;
```

Presently, call the information() capacity to transfer the information on thingspeak cloud. At long last, the significant capacity to call is ESP.deepSleep(); this will make the module to rest for the characterized interim of time which is in microseconds.

```
data();

Serial.println("deep sleep for 15 seconds");

ESP.deepSleep(15e6);
```

Circle capacity will stay unfilled as all the assignment must be performed once and after that reset the module after the characterized interim of time.

Transfer the code in the ESP8266 module. Evacuate the RST and D0 associated wire before transferring the program else it will **give a mistake**.

Testing DeepSleep in the ESP8266

Subsequent to transferring the program you will see that **temperature readings are transferring on the ThingSpeak cloud after like clockwork and after that module go in the profound rest mode.**

This finishes the instructional exercise on utilizing **Deep Sleep in ESP8266 module.** The deepsleep is significant component and it have been incorporated to large majority of the gadgets. You can allude this instructional exercise and apply this strategy for various ventures.

Code

```
// esp8266 deepsleep
#include <ESP8266WiFi.h>
String apiWritekey = "*************";
char ssid[] = "XXXXXXXXXX";  // enter your wifi home router ssid
char password[] = "XXXXXXXXXX"  ;  // enter your wifi home router ssid
char server[] = "api.thingspeak.com";
double tempF;
double tempC;
WiFiClient client;
void connect1() {
  WiFi.disconnect();
  delay(10);
  Serial.print("Connecting to ");
  Serial.println(ssid);
  WiFi.begin(ssid, password);
  while (WiFi.status() != WL_CONNECTED)  {
```

```
    delay(500);
    Serial.print(".");
  }
  Serial.println("");
  Serial.print("NodeMcu connected to wifi...");
}

void data() {
  if (client.connect(server,80))
  {
    String Data = apiWritekey;
        Data +="&field1=";
        Data += String(tempF);
        Data += "\r\n\r\n";

    client.print("POST /update HTTP/1.1\n");
    client.print("Host: api.thingspeak.com\n");
    client.print("Connection: close\n");
    client.print("X-THINGSPEAKAPIKEY:
"+apiWritekey+"\n");
    client.print("Content-Type: application/x-www-form-
urlencoded\n");
    client.print("Content-Length: ");
    client.print(Data.length());
    client.print("\n\n");
```

```
    client.print(Data);
    Serial.println("uploaded to Thingspeak server....");
  }
  client.stop();
}
void setup() {
  Serial.begin(115200);
  Serial.println("device is in Wake up mode");
  while (!Serial) { }
  connect1();
  int value = analogRead(A0);
  float volts=(value/1024.0)*5.0;      //conversion to volts
  tempC = volts*100.0;              //conversion to temp
Celsius
  Serial.print("Temperature C: ");
  Serial.println(tempC);
  data();
  Serial.println("deep sleep for 15 seconds");
  ESP.deepSleep(15e6);
}
void loop() {
}
```

www.ingramcontent.com/pod-product-compliance
Lightning Source LLC
Chambersburg PA
CBHW071113050326
40690CB00008B/1212